"A parent's responsibility is to facilitate the development of their child's consciousness. Thanks to Rona Renner's insightful book, parents now have tools to help accomplish this."

—**Deepak Chopra, MD**

Is That Me Yelling? is a complete and compassionate companion for every parent, educator, and parenting educator.... With excellent examples from her extensive professional and personal experience, nurse Rona illustrates fundamental psychological principles and functional parenting practices with empathy and enthusiasm. Bravo, thanks!"

> —**Marisol Muñoz-Kiehne, PhD**, clinical psychologist, parent
> educator, author, columnist, and former host of *Nuestros Niños*
> radio show (www.nuestrosninos.com)

"As a pediatrician and parent, I truly appreciate Rona Renner's holistic and practical approach to parenting. This book should be required reading for all new parents."

> —**Lawrence Rosen, MD**, founder of The Whole Child Center
> (wholechildcenter.org)

"Engaging and practical, humorous and evidence-based, prescriptive but not preachy, authoritative yet never stuffy, *Is That Me Yelling?* quickly rises to the top of the many parenting books I've ever read. All parents get engaged in power struggles with their kids, and through numerous case examples, easy-to-follow self-assessments, a welcome review of temperament, and just the right dosage of pure wisdom, Rona Renner provides thoughtful and achievable solutions. If you're a parent who has ever yelled at your kid and wished you hadn't, this book is for you."

> —**Stephen P. Hinshaw, PhD**, editor at the *Psychological Bulletin*;
> professor in the department of psychology at the University of
> California, Berkeley; and vice-chair of psychology in the department
> of psychiatry at the University of California, San Francisco

"*Is That Me Yelling?* speaks directly to all of us parents who love our kids with all our hearts, yet still find ourselves losing it. Rona Renner is wise, funny, and right on the mark with this exceptionally useful guide to being the adult in the family."

> —**Katherine Ellison**, author of *Buzz: A Year of Paying Attention and Square Peg: My Story and What It Means for Raising Innovators, Visionaries, and Out-of-the-Box Thinkers*

"Among the many books on parenting, this one stands out for me because it encouraged me to fundamentally change the way I am with my children. With Rona Renner's help, I have stopped yelling and become the patient, compassionate parent I always hoped to be."

> —**Rhonda Collins**, documentary film editor and mother of twins

"There is nothing more heartwarming and healing than a parent striving to be a better parent. *Is That Me Yelling?* is a powerful, loving, and effective book for parents who want to learn how to foster healthier communication and relationships with their children."

> —**Jorge Partida, PsyD**, author of *The Promise of the Fifth Sun* and *A Week of Awakening*

"Yelling doesn't work—at least not for long. Kids get inured to it and stop listening. Then parents have to yell louder, and say more hurtful things. *Is That Me Yelling?* is the best book I've seen on parenting because it shows how to stop the damaging anger and create a spirit of true cooperation with your children. Highly recommended."

> —**Matthew McKay, PhD**, author of *When Anger Hurts Your Kids*

"Finally! An insightful, practical guide that does not shame or preach. *Is That Me Yelling?* provides sensible, easy-to-use techniques using compassion and self-awareness to not only improve ourselves as parents and grandparents, but to also obtain desired behavior changes in our children. This refreshing go-to guide is destined to become indispensable, filling a void in current parenting literature."

> —**Shoshana Bennett, PhD**, clinical psychologist, parental depression specialist, and author of *Postpartum Depression for Dummies*

"Rona Renner counseled me through my early parenting with a very spirited child, and saved us both from much heartbreak and disaster! That *was* me yelling—until I learned the skills and approaches her book offers. What a gift to parents, and to their children!"

—**Betsy Rose**, mindful educator, musician, and parent

"*Is That Me Yelling?* is a funny, warm, and insightful book by a funny, warm, and insightful person. Rona Renner is a beloved speaker, writer, and radio personality known as the go-to person for Bay Area families. Finally, she has put her years of parenting wisdom into a book for all of us. I highly recommend it!"

—**Joshua Coleman, PhD**, psychologist and author of
When Parents Hurt

"I have known and worked with Rona Renner for over several decades. Clearly, she understands that no single behavioral approach fits all children. Instead, each approach must take into account the particular temperament of the child—and often also that of the parent! In this respect, *Is That Me Yelling?* sums up a significant portion of Rona's learning curve…. So parents, if what *should* work doesn't, if *your* pressure gauge is 'way up'—this is the book for you!"

—**James Cameron, PhD**, executive director at The Preventive Ounce,
a nonprofit, preventive mental health organization for children
(preventiveoz.org)

"*Is That Me Yelling?* is simply a gift for parents. Filled with wisdom but delivered with both humor and humility, this book is of value for families in need of minor adjustments, major overhauls, and everything in between. Renner challenges us without judging. The clarity of the writing belies just how transformative these practical recommendations can be for our children and for ourselves."

—**David C. Rettew, MD**, associate professor of psychiatry and
pediatrics, director of the Child & Adolescent Psychiatry Fellowship,
and director of the Pediatric Psychiatry Clinic at the University
of Vermont, College of Medicine

"When it comes to aiding and supporting parents in the care of their children, I believe most caregivers want honest, straightforward, and uncomplicated suggestions from someone who has been there and done that. Rona Renner's book, *Is That Me Yelling?* is a breath of fresh air. Authentic, helpful, easy-to-read, and useful are words that describe her messages to parents as well as professionals."

> —**Intisar Shareef, EdD**, cochair of the Early Childhood Education
> Department at Contra Costa College, San Pablo, CA

"Rona Renner's approach is warm, practical, and wise. She provides a sturdy helping hand for even the toughest situations. Based on real-life experiences, this book is full of sensitive, sound advice that truly works. It should be mandatory reading for every parent."

> —**Mary Sheedy Kurcinka, EdD**, author of *Raising Your Spirited Child*
> and *Sleepless in America*

"The future will be defined by the generation we are raising right now. In the face of global challenges, we must remember that we, as parents, shape the future one decision at a time. Our children will be the ones to reinvent society, business, and humanity's relationship with the natural world. They are the innovators and the peacemakers; the caretakers and the stewards; the visionaries and the implementers. It is our duty to our children and to the planet to give them the best start possible. This begins with knowing ourselves, healing our families, and acting intentionally. As Renner eloquently states, "world peace begins at home.""

> —**Rinaldo S. Brutoco**, futurist, business leader,
> and founding president of the World Business Academy

"*Is That Me Yelling?* is a great way to bring guidance from the wise and warm Nurse Rona into your home. With extensive experience as a nurse, temperament counselor, parent educator, and parenting radio host, her advice is valuable for anyone with kids. Regardless of how much they yell, moms and dads are certain to feel more calm and confident having her by their side."

> —**Will Courtenay, PhD**, "The Men's Doc" and author of
> *Dying to Be Men.*

Is That Me Yelling?

A Parent's Guide

to Getting Your
Kids to Cooperate
Without Losing
Your Cool

Rona Renner, RN

New Harbinger Publications, Inc.

Publisher's Note

Distributed in Canada by Raincoast Books

Copyright © 2014 by Rona Renner
New Harbinger Publications, Inc.
5674 Shattuck Avenue
Oakland, CA 94609
www.newharbinger.com

Cover design by Sara Christian
Text design by Michele Waters-Kermes
Acquired by Tesilya Hanauer
Edited by Gretel Hakanson

Library of Congress Cataloging-in-Publication Data on file

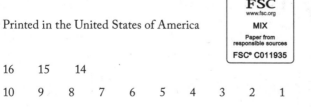

Printed in the United States of America

16   15   14

10   9   8   7   6   5   4   3   2   1

First printing

This book is dedicated to my children, Pay, Mara, Matt, and Carina; to my husband, Mick; and to my grandsons, David and Maceo. Thank you all for opening my heart and continuing to teach me what it means to love.

Contents

Why I Yell at My Kids

Christine Carter, PhD
Author, *Raising Happiness*
September 2013

It was an afternoon like any other. I'd picked my kids up from their after-school activities, and we were driving to dinner at my sister-in-law's house. Because I'd left work an hour early, I still had some calls to make.

I figured I'd make the calls in the car while driving to dinner. The upside of rush hour traffic was that there'd be plenty of time. Since I mostly write from home in a room off our kitchen, I'm well-practiced at working while keeping an ear out for my kids and, in this case, an eye on the road.

I put on an audiobook for the kids and used voice recognition to dial my first call, which went to voicemail. As I was leaving a long message, my kids started talking to me at the same time, asking me to turn up the volume on the audiobook. I find it hugely irritating when my kids can hear that I'm talking to someone else but they start talking to me anyway.

"Can't you hear that I was leaving a message?!" I yelled at them. "Can *you* hear and respond to someone who is talking to you while *you* are talking to someone else?!" I was getting going, fueled by the day's stresses. "I HATE IT WHEN YOU TALK TO ME WHEN I'M ALREADY TALKING TO SOMEONE ELSE! IT MAKES ME FEEL CRAZY! AND IT MAKES ME SOUND SO UNPROFESSIONAL!"

And then, in my headset, I heard a long beep, and a computerized voice told me that I'd reached the end of the length of the message and that the call would now end. Holy crow: I'd been yelling at my kids *right into* my colleague's voicemail. Talk about sounding unprofessional!

My kids don't usually cower (or suddenly obey) when I yell. When I get angry or snappish with them, they say things like, "Mom, could you please use a kind voice?" or even "I have a hard time understanding you when you talk to me like that." Both of these phrases they've stolen directly from me; it's what I say to *them* when they are demanding or disrespectful or whiny to get them to change their tone of voice.

But I don't have a history of changing my own tone in response to their polite or sassy requests. Instead, I've justified yelling at my kids. It's different from when they talk to me in a way that I don't like—because I'm the parent. Moms and dads yell when kids make us mad. Kids need to not do the things that make us yell, and then we won't yell anymore. Ergo, if I'm yelling, clearly it is *the kids'* fault, and therefore, it's *their* responsibility to change.

Except I always knew, on some level, that this is faulty logic. The embarrassment of yelling at my kids in front of a work colleague provided the jolt of insight I needed to see that my yelling couldn't be justified. Moreover, yelling at my kids wasn't actually changing their behavior. Although we all know that yelling occasionally works in the short run, generally speaking, it is not an effective teaching tool. As a parenting expert, I'm very well versed in much more effective ways to shape kids' behavior and habits.

Rona Renner's *Is That Me Yelling?* provided me with the framework that I needed to discover why I was *really* yelling at my kids as well as tools for responding differently in the future. I discovered, by using the Yelling Tracker in chapter 5, that I really only raise my voice with my kids when I'm multitasking—when I'm really focused on something besides them. Working from home or from the car means that I'm often trying to do two or even three things at once, and this dramatically shortens my fuse.

I worked out a plan to work less in the presence of my kids and to give them my full attention when I'm with them. They still do things that make me angry; the difference is that I am much more able and likely to respond skillfully to their missteps when I'm not trying to do something else at the same time.

Is That Me Yelling? makes an important contribution to the betterment of humanity. When we are compassionate and peaceful with our children, they, in turn, become compassionate and peaceful in the world. And in a world filled with strife and irritants, this is just what we need!

Introduction

You're Not Alone

Some years ago, my daughter Carina was downstairs yelling at her brother Matt to stop bothering her. Angrily running to the stairs, I immediately responded at the top of my lungs, "Carina, stop yelling!" In that moment—certainly not the first of such moments—I suddenly heard myself: *Is that* me *yelling?* I was appalled. I was a nurse, a parenting expert; I knew better. That day, I promised myself that I would try to stop doing things that I didn't want my kids to do, starting with yelling. I came to see that my actions were not always the best approach for my children, but when I paid attention and made efforts, over time I learned from my mistakes. After all, I had stopped smoking, and I could stop yelling too!

Parents find themselves yelling at their kids for a lot of reasons. Maybe you were raised by a yeller, and you can't seem to kick the habit of letting your feelings spill out and land on your kids. Now, you want to rid yourself of some traditions that you just don't think are healthy for you or your family.

Or perhaps you're under a lot of stress and have temporarily lost or misplaced your compassion, kindness, and gratitude. This happens easily during parenthood—even though you've discovered deep wells of love for your children at the same time.

Since I first became a parent in 1970, I've learned that we all make mistakes, that there is no such thing as a perfect parent, and that parents love their children. We have the best of intentions, but we are all limited by what we know how to do.

You *Can* Learn to Stop Yelling at Your Kids

Most parents yell at their children occasionally. Losing it with our kids comes with the territory of parenting—we're tired, they're tired, it happens. We can apologize, laugh together, and get back to our calm and patient approach to child rearing. But if you are becoming aware that you are "yelling just like my mother used to yell at us" or "yelling so hard that my throat hurts" or "yelling because I don't know what else to do to make them listen," take heart: you are not alone.

The number one question parents ask me in seminars is this: "How can I stop yelling at my kids all the time?" My guess is that you picked up this book because that's your question too. You already know that the kind of yelling you do isn't good for you or your family, which means you are already on your way to yelling less. Parents are often not likely to talk about the shame they may feel for how often they yell or their despair over their inability to rein in their own impulses even as they ask their kids to control themselves. But these are commonly felt issues.

I have found that combining an understanding of temperament (a person's behavioral style) and a cognitive behavioral approach (working with thoughts, feelings, and actions) works well for parents who are motivated to understand themselves and to make positive changes. Fortunately, we can learn from our mistakes and change our habits and conditioning. And that's what this book is all about.

Here's what you'll learn:

- Why parents yell and what motivates them to change

- The effect of yelling on children and adults

- The day-to-day triggers that set you on the yelling path

- How to recognize the underlying triggers that impact yelling

- How your unique temperament and your child's unique temperament contribute to yelling

- Why you want to stop yelling

- How to yell less—starting right away

You may have picked up this book to help someone else who yells too much—your spouse or partner, or another trusted person in your life who helps to raise your kids. You have come to the right place for help. Although you can't change another person—only he or she can do that—how you act or react will have a powerful impact on the people around you.

Telling your spouse or partner that *she* has to read this book because *she* has a yelling problem is not an approach I recommend! Reading it yourself and offering to read it together to see what common ground you discover might be a better way to start.

It's Never Too Late to Start Fresh

My intention for this book is to give you inspiration and tools to help you yell less, understand yourself better, and forgive yourself for the mistakes you've made and for the ones you will inevitably make in the future. It's never too late to start fresh. As you begin to yell less, you will see and feel the enormous positive impact this change has on your health and happiness. And you will be giving your children a gift that will be passed on to future generations.

Parents who are concerned that they yell too often are relieved to know that other people struggle with similar issues. This book offers many stories that I hope will resonate with you, but it does not provide you with a room filled with like-minded parents. You might find it beneficial to talk about these issues with friends or family as you learn more.

My expertise has come from my education and training, from raising my four children, from watching my grandchildren grow, and from the thousands of parents and teachers like you who have come to my classes, listened to my radio shows, and reached out to me for individual advice and support. When I worked in the Pediatric Department at Kaiser Permanente, Richmond Medical Center, I had the privilege of helping parents learn new skills and approaches to raising children. Through their stories, I learned about their cultures, traditions, and struggles.

It is possible to have more harmony at home, and I am grateful to have the opportunity to pass on some of what I've learned as a daughter, mother, wife, nurse, temperament counselor, trainer, radio show host, and observer of people. When I think about the complex world issues that face us and the generations to come, I find myself repeating the words "world peace begins at home." By reading this book, you are not only doing something valuable for yourself and for your kids, you are truly helping to change the world—one family at a time.

Rona Renner, RN
Berkeley, California
August 2013

Part 1

Understanding Yelling

The chapters in this section are designed to help you understand why you yell and how yelling impacts everyone in the family. Before you can help your children change their behaviors, you need to take a compassionate look at yourself. Benjamin Franklin, in his *Poor Richard's Almanac*, addressed this challenge: "There are three things extremely hard: steel, a diamond, and to know one's self."

It may be hard, but you can do it!

You may be tempted to skip ahead to part 2, where I discuss solutions, but I urge you to take the time to read all of the chapters in part 1. Becoming an expert on yourself and your child will help you tackle new problems as they arise.

Chapter 1

"Is That Me Yelling?"

Becoming Aware of Yourself

"Without warning my son throws his toy car at his sister. She begins to cry, and he begins to laugh. The next thing I know, I'm yelling at the top of my lungs. I tell my son how sick and tired I am of his behavior and what a mean kid he's become. Now both kids are crying and hiding under the table. I hate the out-of-control parent I've become."

—Jennifer, mother of a five-year-old son
and a three-year-old daughter

Your wish to change is a gift to you and your family.

Many parents have told me that their desire to change came when they finally realized that they were not being patient or compassionate and that yelling was setting a bad example for their kids. They also saw that yelling wasn't effective: it did not reduce their child's misbehavior over time.

Realizing that you want to yell less and that you can do something about your automatic reactions is the first step on the path to change.

How to Know When You're Yelling (and When You're Not)

When parents yell—regardless of their volume—they are usually angry or frustrated and have lost some degree of control. If you check in with yourself, you can tell the difference pretty easily. For example, when I yelled at my kids, I always felt my intensity rising—my breathing was up, my heart rate was up, and I was literally feeling hot under the collar. I was no longer thinking clearly. My main goal was to express my frustration and let my kids know that they had better listen "or else."

In contrast, the assertive communication you use thoughtfully as a part of the way you discipline is *not* the same as yelling. Being firm and calm is frequently a good way to get your child to listen to your requests. It is *not* yelling when you tell your child what you expect and what the consequences will be if he doesn't do what you've asked.

A Nonyelling Example

Here is a nonyelling example: Olivia is playing happily on the floor, and her mother, Nora, squats down to her level. With a firm voice Nora says to her daughter, "It's time to put your clothes on for school. I know you like playing, but the timer went off." When Olivia continues to play and doesn't respond, Nora continues in a firm tone, "If you are late for school today, there won't be a playdate this afternoon. Will you get dressed yourself, or do you need some help?"

Nora's tone of voice and attitude is key here. The same words could be said in a loud or harsh voice with a threatening tone, or they could be said with a firm and calm tone. If the goal is to criticize your child for not getting dressed and making you late, you might quickly transition into yelling. But if the goal is to help her learn about the morning routine, then staying calm is essential. If Nora started yelling as soon as she saw her daughter wasn't dressed, chances are that Olivia would focus on feelings such as fear or anger rather than the act of getting her clothes on. Her feelings might trigger a stress response and cause her to cry, withdraw, or tune out. Getting dressed in the morning could become a battle that mother and daughter fight every day.

Yelling is usually a way to let children know that you're mad at them or something they did. Yelling is usually not about teaching; it's about stopping behavior by intimidation or fear, and it's about expressing your negative feelings. How loud you yell will vary, but there is always an exaggerated intensity.

Being Firm When Needed

I once took care of a friend's child who had trouble listening to the requests of adults. He was a sweet three-year-old boy who had a mind of his own. One day, we were walking on a busy street, and he ran ahead of me. I called for him to come back, but he kept going even though I knew he heard me. I caught up with him, got down to his level, looked him in the eyes, and said in a loud but controlled voice, "Don't ever run away from me again."

I was firm, but I was not out of control. I wanted him to feel the force of my statement so he would understand that what he had done was not acceptable and not safe. For this child, who often tuned people out, it was an effective approach. When he started to cry, I made sure to give him a hug and tell him how much I cared about him and why it was important for him to stay with me. He was comforted, and we went on our way. I let his mom know what happened so she could follow up as needed.

The art of parenting is an improvisation that is fluid and always changing. If you put the physical and emotional needs of your children at the center of your discipline and if you practice staying aware of your thoughts, your emotions, and your breathing, with a little luck, you will raise healthy and happy children. It's up to you to decide when yelling is appropriate and when to rethink your discipline approaches. Your relationship with your children is for a lifetime.

Is Yelling Ever Appropriate?

Opinions vary about when it's appropriate to yell. You'll have to grapple with this question after observing the impact of your yelling. Most people I've talked to think it's appropriate to yell sometimes, especially in dangerous situations when someone might get hurt—to stop a child who is reaching for the hot stove or about to dash into a busy street.

Here are some examples of when I think yelling is appropriate:

- If you see a car coming when your child is crossing the street and you don't think he's looking, a loud yell might be just what he needs to stop in time. (*Don't* go on and on yelling about what might have happened.)

- If your older child is about to feed the baby some peanuts and you're not close enough to stop her, a shout of "No, don't do that!" might work well. This is especially effective if yelling is not your default method of communication.

- If your grandson spills water near your computer, you might yell loudly, "Oh no, get the towel!" In this case you're not yelling at the child, you are reacting to prevent a fried computer. (A note of caution: If you're in a bad mood, you might start to yell in a blaming way about the spilled water. Thoughts such as *Why can't he be more careful?* might fuel your yelling. We'll talk about trigger thoughts in chapter 2.)

EXERCISE: Why Parents Want to Yell Less

The parents who come to my workshops are probably a lot like you. They love their children, work hard at being good parents, and do their best at managing a home, a business, or both. Many of the parents I've talked with were raised by yellers. These parents are surprised to find themselves yelling, because they made a promise to themselves not to imitate their parents and not to yell or express mean words to their kids. But somehow, it just comes out.

Some people have told me that they had unrealistic expectations about what it takes to raise a child. They had limited experience with kids before becoming a parent and didn't understand the time, money, and emotional commitment needed.

The following list of reasons parents want to stop yelling was gathered from the classes I've taught over the years. Review the list and check off the reasons you identify with. Add your reasons to the list.

☐ *My dad yelled and was verbally abusive. I don't want to be like him.*

☐ *My daughter doesn't listen when I yell; she tunes me out.*

☐ *I want to model respectful behavior.*

☐ *I want to be a better parent than I am right now.*

☐ *I want to teach my kids to be good at resolving conflicts.*

☐ *I've started to yell even when my son's friends are around.*

☐ *I don't like how I feel when I yell.*

☐ *I hated it when my parents yelled.*

☐ *I feel guilty and ashamed when I yell and say angry things.*

☐ *I want to break the cycle of yelling in my family.*

☐ *I don't want to see the look of fear on my child's face.*

☐ *I heard my son mumble, "Mama doesn't love me anymore."*

☐ *My daughter imitates me.*

☐ *When I yell, it means I'm not good at my job.*

☐ *Yelling drains my energy.*

☐ *My kids yell at each other.*

☐ *I'm afraid it will lead me to hitting my kids.*

☐ *My neighbors give me dirty looks.*

☐ *My kids run to my partner when I yell, because they're afraid of me.*

☐ *I feel like a mean dad.*

☐ *I want to stop yelling because of the look on my child's face.*

☐ *I don't want to damage my child.*

☐ *Yelling makes me hate myself.*

☐ *My wife told me I have to yell less.*

☐ *I'm scared of my own yelling. It's as if I become another person.*

☐ *My partner is afraid of me when I yell at the kids.*

☐ *I don't want my kids to experience shame.*

☐ _____

☐ _____

Take some time to think about the role yelling has in your life. Use this list to help you reflect on your desire to yell less.

How Yelling Affects Children

As you deepen your desire to yell less and as you prepare to make changes, an important piece of the puzzle is to consider the impact of yelling on children. In the list of reasons why you want to yell less, there are some examples of the consequences of yelling. Statements like "I don't want to see the look of fear on my child's face" and hearing your child say, "Mama doesn't love me anymore" are powerful incentives for change. We will come back to the specific consequences for *your* children, but first we'll take a look at how yelling impacts the mental health of children in general.

Most professionals agree that yelling has an impact on a child's feelings about themselves, their world, and the relationships they have with their parents and others. According to psychologist Myrna B. Shure (2005), when parents discipline by yelling and commanding, their children are more likely to show physical or verbal aggression. These children will have more difficulty with positive social behaviors such as taking turns and empathizing with other children.

The Words You Say Matter

When considering the impact of yelling on children, consider the frequency, duration, and intensity of the yelling and the actual words you use to express your feelings. For example, yelling at a child from the other room, "I said to stop jumping on the couch!" is different from yelling, "You're such a wild brat. I told you not to jump on the couch! Why can't you behave like your sister?" In this example, a child is being told that he is bad, and he's likely to interpret his parent's words to mean that his sister is loved more.

What Are Most Days Like?

Another factor to consider is what your family life is like most of the time. Do you usually enjoy open communication, fun together, and a sense of love and trust? Or is there frequent tension, arguing, and a high stress level for all? If there is daily arguing and stress, then it's essential to put time and energy into slowly making shifts in family priorities. Your meaningful connections will help to balance out times of conflict as you are learning to yell less.

Many Parents Are Yellers

Research shows that a high percentage of parents admit to yelling at their young children and to expressing psychological aggression toward them (Straus and Field 2003). So rest assured: you are not alone.

It's safe to assume that most of your friends and relatives also yell at their kids, but they may not want to talk about it due to feelings of embarrassment or incompetence. In some ways yelling has become the "new spanking." Because of the research on the negative consequences of spanking, many parents have made the decision not to physically hurt or hit their children but haven't learned what to do instead. Since there is a good chance you were raised by at least one parent who yelled, it's easy to resort to yelling as the go-to form of discipline.

Be forewarned: yelling at children on a regular basis will set them up for more challenges during the turbulent teenage years. Research presented in the book *When Anger Hurts Your Kids* shows that "the amount of anger expressed in the family will affect your child's performance in nearly every important area of his or her adolescent life. Anger casts a long shadow, blighting not just the moment, but the emotional, academic, and social functioning of your child" (Tesser et al. 1989; McKay et al. 1996, 6).

13

If your child had a yelling match with you before leaving the house for school, his attention to detail on his early morning English test might be compromised by his physiological and emotional responses to the anger you both expressed. I know that when I've had an argument with my husband, my ability to think clearly and make work-related decisions is impaired until I can calm and soothe myself or apologize for my reactions. It takes insight and practice to understand and let go of hurt feelings.

Anger is a normal emotion and is something everyone feels. There is nothing wrong with feeling angry. In fact, your anger can help you understand what's working and not working in your life. It can also motivate you to take a stand at work, address a miscommunication, or clean out a messy garage. If you feel angry every time your teenager leaves her dishes on the table and walks away without saying thank you, your anger serves as a message that something needs to change. In that case, it might be time for a heart-to-heart talk with your teen about the value of developing an attitude of gratitude.

The practices you'll learn in this book will help you become aware of your negative feelings and manage the range of emotions that lead to yelling when your child misbehaves or just acts her age. The stakes are too high to continue to yell on a regular basis. You are missing too many good days filled with connection, respect, and love.

Assess the Effect of Yelling on *Your* Child

Now that you've read about some of the negative consequences of yelling in general, it's time to see how yelling affects *your* child. All children are different, and one of the tasks of being a parent is to become an expert on your own child. If you are willing to observe yourself and your child, it can lead to living with more joy and pleasure, and you will have an easier time knowing what to do when your child misbehaves.

I admit that there were many times when I had blinders on, when I didn't want to see the consequences of my actions or inaction. It took me a long time (and I still work on this) to be courageous enough to see things as they are and to be kind to myself at the same time. If you can quiet your overly critical thoughts, you will learn a tremendous amount.

If your self-critic is fully employed, you will be less likely to want to notice the not-so-attractive side of yourself.

For an entire year I did an exercise where I kissed my hand and said, "I'm good" every time I made a mistake and when I heard myself say something negative about myself (internally or externally). I felt awkward and silly at first, but it was a concrete way for me to increase my compassion toward myself. It takes practice to treat yourself with kindness. And the more you direct loving kindness toward yourself and others, the more relaxed and aware you will become. I mention this now because as you observe your child, feelings such as sadness, remorse, or guilt may arise. This step of observing the consequences of yelling at your child is vital to your goal of yelling less. You are making a commitment to learn the truth.

EXERCISE: Observe Your Child

Your goal in this exercise is to learn about your child's response to your yelling. Don't change what you normally do, just observe the impact it has. If you have already started to yell less, think about the consequences you observed in the past.

How children react depends on many factors, including their temperament. For example, if your son is sensitive, your look of disappointment and your yelling tone might affect him for hours. You may find that he's quiet in the car and doesn't want to kiss you goodbye. When he should focus on his math, he can't because he is preoccupied with the fact that you yelled and called him selfish. A child who is sensitive is often highly perceptive and can easily internalize negative emotions. Another child, who is intense and high in energy, might yell back at you and then go off to school and have a decent day. She may even seem to enjoy a yelling match first thing in the morning, with you or with her little sister.

Temperament is a person's natural style of responding to people, places, and events. You move in the world based on many inborn traits. In chapter 4 you will learn about your child's temperament and your own. Understanding how well your temperment matches your child's will help you reduce power struggles and yelling.

In this exercise you get to be an amateur sociologist as you learn about your child during the week. Write down what you notice about your child after you have yelled or spoken harshly. Use a journal or your computer to take notes. You will be able to go back to your notes when you need a reminder later on of why you are making the effort to change your yelling habit. Remember, the goal here is to observe your child during and after yelling. Don't focus your attention at this time on your actions, triggers, or feelings. That will come later.

Children respond to yelling in various ways. Below you will find typical responses. Check off the ones you identify with, and make notes of your observations.

My child

☐ *tunes out my yelling;*

☐ *looks frightened when I yell;*

☐ *says something like, "You don't love me anymore";*

☐ *imitates me and starts to yell;*

☐ *runs crying to Mommy;*

☐ *yells at friends and even the cat;*

☐ *hides under the table and won't come out until I promise I'll stop;*

☐ *has trouble separating from me after I've yelled;*

☐ *comes home from school in a bad mood and goes right to his room;*

☐ *tells me to use my inside voice;*

☐ *laughs when I yell until I threaten to spank;*

☐ *mopes around the house;*

☐ *can't get to sleep after I've yelled;*

☐ *plays hitting and punching games with her stuffed animals;*

☐ *listens to me only when I yell;*

☐ *doesn't seem bothered by my yelling;*

☐ *doesn't bring his school friends over anymore;*

☐ *does what I've yelled at her to do;*

☐ _____

Stick With It!

Making observations about the effect of yelling on your child is difficult, but stick with it: this practice will increase your feelings of empathy and guide you in your parenting practices. For example, if you see that your child has become immune to being yelled at, you will have more resolve to develop a new approach. If you see that your daughter has become a champion yeller, you will get the clear message that it's time to model a different kind of communication.

Be kind to yourself as you do this exercise. As you become familiar with yourself and develop more self-acceptance, your kindness toward your child will also grow.

Carla, a mother of twins, told me about an observation she made that confirmed her deep desire to stop yelling. "This morning Felicia said to her dolly, 'I'm getting angry at you.' She hit the doll and shouted over and over, 'Go to sleep!'" Hearing this was painful for Carla but also vital to her efforts to change the nightly struggles at bedtime.

No parent wants to teach his or her child how to yell, except in dangerous situations. Since you are your child's first teacher, think about what kind of education you want to provide. Your frequent yelling can overshadow important life skills and lessons that you teach your child every day.

What Would Your Child Tell You?

If your child could express how yelling affects her, what do you think she would say?

At a home visit I made in a professional capacity, I asked a seven-year-old boy, "If you had a magic wand and you could make a wish to change something about your father, what would it be?" He replied without hesitation, "I wish that he didn't yell anymore. At me or my mom." His father's stern face softened as he listened to his son and held back his tears. He made a commitment then and there to do more about managing his anger and working on his marriage.

Being honest with yourself and observing what goes on in your family is a vital and difficult task. Recognizing mistakes and the consequences of your actions while being compassionate toward yourself is not something most people have been taught to do. Doing this work is like learning a new language or sport. You need tools, support from others, patience, a desire to reach your goals, and a willingness to make mistakes. As you read this book, find a person you trust and can share some of your insights with.

Being a "Good Enough" Parent

When I first began to notice how my yelling affected my kids, I felt lousy about the job I was doing as a mother. I thought it meant that I had failed and that I would never learn how to get good at the one job I wanted to master more than any other. Over the years I came to see that I would frequently feel insecure and frustrated and that new challenges were always just around the corner. With practice I learned how to reduce my yelling and name-calling and to recognize the good instincts I had as a mother. I observed the teachers in my children's co-op preschools and learned how they got kids to cooperate without yelling. I read about child development to understand what was normal for different ages, and I talked to other parents to learn from them. I came to see I wasn't the only one feeling confused. This book encapsulates what I learned. It will show you how you too can be a good enough parent, learn to tolerate the feelings of not knowing what to do, and respond rather than react to your child's behavior. There is no such thing as perfection when it comes to parenting. So celebrate the good moments and learn from the hard ones. It's never too late to make changes.

No Blaming, No Shaming

Knowing why you want to yell less and understanding the consequences your yelling has on your children will motivate you to yell less. So it's essential that you be honest with yourself, without shame or blame.

When you start to feel guilty or ashamed because you have yelled, think of something you can say to yourself to reframe your negative thoughts. Instead of thinking, *I've damaged my kids for life,* try replacing that thought with *I'm doing the best I can, and I'll keep learning more* or *It's never too late to change.* Take time to notice your feelings and thoughts and then find the words to substitute that are right for you. If you repeat negative thoughts about yourself, you are likely to feel bad and diminish your motivation to change. Your thoughts really do matter, and not being hard on yourself is an attitude worth developing.

When I had young children, I frequently criticized myself for not knowing what to do and at times thought I was a bad mother. When this happened I would in turn become more critical of the people around me, especially my children. Self-criticism and shame are not the same as taking your own measure, feeling regret, forgiving yourself, and coming to understand what you can do differently. Learn to be your own cheerleader, rooting for your success and being enthusiastic about your efforts.

Using the Cognitive Behavioral Approach

In the example above I have asked you to change your thinking in order to change what you feel. This reflects the cognitive behavioral therapy (CBT) approach that many therapists use, which I've come to value. I first learned about this approach from the book *When Anger Hurts Your Kids* (McKay et al. 1996) when I was working with Matthew McKay on a *20/20* TV episode about parental anger. This type of treatment helps people understand more about the thoughts and feelings that influence their behaviors.

One of the reasons this approach is so powerful is that you have the capacity to notice and then change your thoughts in order to feel better and react differently to stressful situations. Observing your thoughts, noticing and identifying emotions, and tracking your actions is key to yelling less. I have witnessed the benefit of this approach with many parents.

Right now, you can start to become aware of your negative thoughts and substitute something positive. I remember a time when I felt anxious on a turbulent airplane ride. I realized that instead of saying to myself, *I'm going to die, and I will never see my kids again,* I could replace that repetitive thought with a simple, more positive (and more likely) statement: *This too shall pass. I'll be just fine.* Within no time, repeating these comforting words helped me feel less anxious. In the next chapter, you will learn how easy it is for your thoughts to trigger your emotions and set off your yelling.

But I Want to Yell Less *Now*!

Change *can* happen quickly, but it is usually a slow and steady process.

Around thirty years ago I had a moment of clarity when I knew I should stop smoking for good. I had always stopped when I was pregnant, but smoking helped me focus and relax, so I would start again once my baby stopped nursing. With my third child, I had a craving to smoke before my son was ready to give up nursing. I took a puff of a cigarette from a friend, and instantly, I felt my heart skip a beat—not the good feeling of your heart skipping a beat when you fall in love, but the scary feeling of an irregular heartbeat. I immediately associated inhaling the smoke with damaging my heart and dying while my children were still young. That did it for me. I vowed to give up smoking, and I did.

Sometimes motivation, insight, and change can happen quickly, as it did for me at that moment. But it usually takes support, missteps, patience, practice, and persistence over time. It's not like smoking or not smoking—you can't always catch yourself when a request to put toys away starts to morph into a yelling match. Giving up cigarettes was easier for me than learning to manage my anger and frustration when I was faced with misbehaving kids who triggered me to act in ways I didn't want to.

It's important to remember that your yelling is just *one* part of how you are as a parent. You are not yelling at your child twenty-four hours a day. Take a moment to bring to mind a recent time when you were compassionate, loving, and responsive to your child. What did you do? How did you feel? Take a minute to picture the situation and the positive consequences for your child and for yourself. This experience can be a blueprint for a future of increased harmony at home.

I remember a day when my son started to pick on his sister (which he often did). Instead of yelling (which I often did then), I said something like, "Matt, did someone pick on you today?" He stopped and looked sad, and I knew he needed a hug and time to talk about what he had dealt with at school. His behavior had meaning, and I was calm enough to see that. He also needed to understand that picking on his sister wouldn't solve his difficulties.

Your desire to yell less will be informed by the observed and imagined consequences for you and your children. My desire to stop smoking came when I realized that my health was at risk; my wish to not yell at my kids came when I saw that I was modeling responses that I disapproved of and did not want to perpetuate. An honest assessment frees you to move forward.

In the next chapter, you will learn about *self-observation*. This art of paying attention to yourself will help you observe the way you move, react, breathe, speak, and feel. It's done with compassion and a desire to see things as they are, without judgment. It's so much easier to be calm and less reactive to your kids once you've taken stock of the kinds of behaviors and situations that set you on the warpath.

A Thought to Consider:
Yelling comes easily to me.

Even though you know that yelling isn't the best way to discipline your child, notice how often you resort to it. Yelling happens so fast, without much effort or planning. Keep paying attention to the impact it has on your child and on you. Is it working to accomplish what you want?

Yelling may come easily, but so do the deep concern and love you have for your child. Picture how you will feel when yelling doesn't come easily anymore.

Chapter 2

"Why Am I Yelling?"
Understanding Everyday Triggers

"I never imagined that I would have a child who talks back to me and thinks she's the boss of everyone. How did that happen, and what am I supposed to do now?"

—Brice, psychologist and parent of a
seven-year-old

Years ago, I read a popular parenting book that offered specific techniques and things to say to get my kids to listen to me. I was surprised and disappointed to discover that when I attempted to follow the instructions, I actually yelled more and felt worse about myself. I think this happened because, despite my efforts and the book's well-intentioned ideas, I did not pay attention to what was triggering my yelling. The book-driven responses to my children were inauthentic, and my children responded by testing me more.

In this chapter you'll identify the everyday occurrences that trigger your yelling, and you'll also discover how your body feels and reacts when you're about to lose your cool. Once you identify the triggers that come from your children, daily circumstances, your thoughts, and your feelings, you'll be ready to focus on the changes that are needed.

As you continue to read this book, you will discover ways to become more familiar with the unique temperaments and responses of both yourself and your children. In this chapter we will explore the kinds of everyday triggers that can set off your yelling before you even know what happened. As you gather this self-knowledge, you will begin to be able to tolerate the times when you don't know what to do. You will become more creative and responsive in how you choose to discipline. And you will experiment and make decisions based on your understanding and love for yourself and your children.

Everyday Yelling Triggers That Set You Off

Tracy, the parent of a four-year-old and a seven-year-old, told me, "Four in the afternoon is my meltdown hour. I wish I could make it without yelling until five, when my wife comes home. The kids are tired and cranky, and really get into picking on each other. I need some peace and quiet by the end of the day, but instead, I get whining, fighting, and a headache."

Kristen, a mommy blogger and the mother of two young daughters, said, "I hate when I'm trying to clean the house and get ready to leave, and then I see that one of the kids has been dismantling one room while I'm tidying another. It gives me that feeling that I can't get ahead. Yes, I'm a neat freak. You never know if you'll bump into the Queen at the grocery store and decide to have her over for tea!"

Observing the circumstances and time of day when you are most likely to yell is courageous and worthwhile. You have unique triggers, and there are also common hot-button everyday events that get parents moving down the yelling path. In Tracy's case, a plan is needed for something different to take place during the witching hour. This family is in overload mode. There's a good chance that they are all tired from a full day of adapting to the demands of their environment, controlling their impulses, and working hard. As a family they need to rethink the afternoons and come up with strategies and plans that will reduce the stress for everyone.

24

Kristen's sense of humor helps her get through some of the rough spots of the day, but she admits that giving up a little bit of her perfectionism would help reduce her yelling.

External Triggers

A *trigger* is a cue or prompt. An *external trigger* comes from something or someone outside of you. An external trigger can be almost anything that calls for you to take action—for example:

- When you're driving and see the brake lights of the car in front of you go on, you know to put your brakes on as well.

- Every time your daughter whines, you get annoyed, and when she goes on for a few minutes you start to yell. The external trigger is her tone of voice and demands.

- When you see your partner has left his underwear on the bathroom floor again, you get angry. His action is a trigger for your emotional response.

You respond to events and people all day long. Your interpretation of an event impacts your emotions and what you do in response.

Escalating Thoughts and Feelings

Before you begin yelling, you will experience *escalating thoughts and feelings*. This is an internal state, as McKay et al. (1996) explain in *When Anger Hurts Your Kids: A Parent's Guide*. According to these authors, there are two elements that precede an expression of anger: stress and trigger thoughts. You may be feeling anxious, afraid, disappointed, or annoyed, or you may be experiencing turbulent thoughts about a current situation that fuels your emotions. An external event may be the initial trigger for angry feelings, but then your thoughts add fuel to the fire. This makes sense to me, but I use the phrase "escalating thoughts and emotions" instead, as the ingredient that mixes with external triggers to cause yelling.

For example, you see your partner's underwear on the floor (external trigger), and you start to say things to yourself (escalating thoughts): *He's such a slob; why do I have to do everything?* or *I've asked him a hundred times to put his stuff in the hamper but he just doesn't care what I want.* You might also experience sadness or anger in response to the thought that he doesn't care enough about you to pick up after himself.

Your feelings will become more intense as you continue to say negative things to yourself. When your partner walks into the room, after your thoughts and feelings have been escalating, you blast him for being an unloving slob. If the kids are around, they may be the next targets on your hit list. The underwear was the external trigger, and then your thoughts escalated your feelings to the point of yelling and expressing anger and hurt.

As you become more familiar with your triggers and escalating thoughts and feelings, you can begin to make changes to prevent yelling. You can't control the challenges that come your way day to day, but you do have control over how you respond and how you interpret what you see, hear, and feel. The cognitive behavioral approach to problem solving and behavior change is quite effective but does take a willingness to reflect on your feelings, thoughts, and behaviors.

Let's look at two stories that illustrate the interplay of external triggers and escalating thoughts. Even if they don't reflect your precise circumstances, you will probably relate to them.

• Nico's Story

Nico is in graduate school and working hard on his dissertation. One night, Nico's six-year-old son, Jason, starts to fuss and refuses to get ready for bed. His complaining annoys Nico and adds to his stress. Almost immediately, Nico moves into familiar thoughts: *He's fussing now just because I have to get my schoolwork done. He's always trying to get more out of me. He's acting like such a baby. He's old enough to get to bed by himself.*

Nico's escalating thoughts increase the resentment he feels, and he expresses his emotions by yelling at Jason: "There won't be any story tonight because of all your fussing.

When are you going to just get ready for bed without making it hard on me? I'm sick of this!"

The consequence of yelling, for Nico, is that he feels bad the rest of the evening. He tries to get his studying done, but he is distracted by feelings of guilt. The consequence for Jason is that he goes to bed crying, and he misses an opportunity to be close to his dad during bedtime. Jason misses Nico after a long day at school. He often feels as if his daddy has more important things to do than to be with him.

If Nico had been able to stop his escalating thoughts, he might have remembered that Jason often has trouble with transitions. A child who is slow to adapt to changes and transitions can easily trigger a parent's impatience. Jason needs help to start his bedtime routine, and when Dad puts music on or tells the "clean-up story," things go much better. Later in the book you'll learn how you can change escalating thoughts that trigger a negative reaction.

• Pat's Story

One day Pat wakes up feeling irritable. She realizes that she won't have time to go to the grocery store before dinner because there's too much to do, so she'll have to get takeout again. She's worried about the meeting she's having with her boss today, and she remembers that her daughter has a soccer game she will miss. She starts to feel like a terrible mother.

Pat really wants to be there for her kids, but she is also trying hard to make a good impression at her new job. Since she and her partner separated, she's been under a tremendous amount of stress.

As Pat rushes around the house getting ready, her kids start to beg her to make Mickey Mouse pancakes for breakfast. She suddenly barks at them, "Who do you think I am, your private chef? Today's a school day, so make your own breakfast!"

As they moan and complain, Pat continues to yell, "Hurry up, because I can't be late today. Don't you know how important it is for me to get to work on time? You're always asking me to buy you things, but if I don't have a job there won't be any money. So hurry up!"

Pat's thoughts about her day and her anxiety about work precede her yelling. Her state of mind is a breeding ground for angry words. The request for pancakes lights the fuse, and she explodes. Pat's children are hurt by her anger and go off to school confused and discouraged.

Pat's story is an example of how thoughts and feelings can start you off in a bad mood, trigger your yelling, and set the tone for your entire day. Pat could have said no without yelling and without making her kids feel as if there was something wrong with them because they had normal childhood desires.

EXERCISE: "That Sets Me Off!" Identifying Common Triggers

Some typical reasons parents yell are fatigue, stress, sibling fighting, and frustration due to noncompliance or unwanted behaviors. There are ample opportunities each day for you to lose your sense of calm and balance.

In the lists below, you will see some common triggers and internal states. Take some time to identify the ones that set you off on a regular basis. You'll find some things will elicit a predictable yelling response from you.

Internal Triggers. *I yell when I feel*

☐ *frustrated.*

☐ *hungry.*

☐ *tired.*

☐ *overwhelmed.*

☐ *lonely.*

- [ ] sad.

- [ ] anxious.

- [ ] misunderstood.

- [ ] resentful.

- [ ] insecure.

- [ ] confused.

- [ ] rushed.

- [ ] embarrassed.

- [ ] impatient.

- [ ] _____

External Triggers. *I yell when my children*

- [ ] fight with each other.

- [ ] don't do what I ask.

- [ ] tune me out.

- [ ] argue with me.

- [ ] whine.

- [ ] have tantrums.

- [ ] don't nap or go to bed on time.

- [ ] don't get up on time.

- [ ] won't get dressed by themselves.

- [ ] take forever to get out of the house.

- [ ] fuss about food and eating.

- [ ] climb all over me and want my attention.

☐ *make too much noise.*

☐ *don't tell the truth.*

☐ *ask questions over and over again.*

☐ *keep doing something even though I've asked them to stop.*

☐ _____

Nonchild External Triggers. *I yell at my children when*

☐ *my spouse doesn't come home on time.*

☐ *I've had a bad day at work.*

☐ *the house is a mess.*

☐ *my partner and I aren't getting along.*

☐ *my mother comes over.*

☐ *we're running late.*

☐ *Grandpa contradicts my discipline.*

☐ *I'm premenstrual.*

☐ _____

Write down some of your triggers in a journal and add new ones as they arise. In future chapters you will use your understanding of yelling triggers to come up with a plan, but for now just continue to become familiar with the things that set you off.

When Yelling Has Become a Habit

For some people, stress and frequent yelling triggers will lead to a habitual yelling response. When a habit develops, you don't think about your behavior, it just happens—like brushing your teeth when you first wake up, kissing your kids good-bye, or always taking your shoes off when you come home. As with other habits, you don't think about what you will or won't do, you just react in a way that you've become accustomed to.

I Just Want Them to Listen to Me

It may feel normal to yell when you want your kids to listen, since it seems to get the job done. You yell a few times, and when you're loud enough, the kids stop arguing. In a way, their response may be training you to keep yelling, since they don't listen unless you raise your voice and yell. Yelling becomes the way things are done in the family. As I said in chapter 1, it's vital that you observe the consequences of your yelling; otherwise, your habit will get stronger. Some habits make our life easier so we can concentrate on more important things, but a yelling habit is harmful to you and your children.

• Saul's Story

Saul, a single father of three young sons, has too much on his plate. He and his kids just moved to a new town, and he has allowed his stress and frustration to become the fuel for his interactions with his sons.

Saul helps his three sons get ready for school. Most mornings his son Noah doesn't want to get up and get dressed. Saul's response is to yell something like, "I've told you three times to get up. If you don't, you're not going to watch any TV tonight. So get the 'bleep' up now!"

When Saul yells, Noah knows it's really time to get up. He doesn't like it when his dad yells, but the extra few minutes of sleep is always so tempting, especially since Noah dreads going to his new school. His brothers hate the morning yelling ritual, and they do whatever they can to avoid their dad's wrath.

Saul's anger and yelling works to get Noah out of bed, and so the habit continues. Chances are that Saul has not yet observed and felt the consequences his yelling has on his relationship with his boys.

Beginning to Break the Habit

Do you have a yelling habit? If so, be kind to yourself—habits are difficult to break. Don't put pressure on yourself to change overnight. Observe your triggers, feelings, and thoughts. Allow yourself to feel and see the consequences of your actions on your kids and on you.

In this case, Saul and Noah could have a heart-to-heart talk about what's going on at school, why Noah is so tired, how hard moving has been, and what routine would work best in the morning. If Saul understood his son's temperament, he would know that transitions are difficult for him and could come up with a plan to help him in the morning. He would also realize how sensitive Noah is and how yelling really makes him feel bad. Saul might be willing to get up early enough so that he has his coffee and breakfast before he has to deal with the kids, which would tone down his intensity. Saul also needs time to reflect on the kind of support he and his children need, now that they are living in a new town without extended family to help.

We'll get into this much more when we talk about temperament in chapter 4 and behavior strategies in part 2.

Breeding Grounds for Yelling

In addition to yelling triggers, several all-too-common situations can really decrease your tolerance for child-parent conflict and increase the likelihood that you'll yell. Chief among them are parental isolation, sleep deprivation, and feeling that you have no time for yourself.

Parental Isolation

Many of the parents I talk with report feeling isolated and unsupported. Often parents have moved away from their family of origin and are raising children without the help of grandparents, aunts, and uncles. With parents working long hours, there is little time to make friends or to reach out to people for support. It takes a village to raise a child, but a large number of parents are raising their children without that safety net. That's what happened to me, years ago.

● Rona's Story

When I moved to San Francisco with my first husband, he was working long hours as a resident physician. After I gave birth, I found myself in a lonely position: I had no friends who were home caring for a baby like I was. Back then, there were few mothers' groups, and there wasn't any online support. I began to feel down and discouraged, which is not my usual nature.

One day, I went to the park and spotted a woman with a baby my son's age sitting by herself. I went over to her and said, "Do you mind if I sit here with you? I'm looking for a friend." She smiled and said something about how lonely it can get in the city with a little baby. We exchanged phone numbers and promised to call soon. We were good friends for many years after that. Having another parent to spend time with changed my mood and helped me be a more patient mother. The frustration and uncertainty I was feeling as a young mother was lessened by having someone to talk to. We often spent late afternoons together making muffins or having a glass of wine and letting our children make a mess and play together.

Isolation may be a trigger for your yelling. If so, be courageous and reach out to other parents at parks, libraries, or your child's school. Most cities have programs where parents can come together. Online parenting groups work well for some people as well.

Sleep Deprivation

If you're an exhausted parent, as most are, you already know you need more sleep. You feel it every day as you doze off at work, forget to do things, or yell at your kids. There are many consequences of too little sleep, such as lack of focus, irritability, poor emotional control, an overall foggy feeling, and a weakened immune system. The American Psychological Association reported on research and a pilot study that shows that the quality of mothers' sleep was a significant predictor of their mood, stress, and fatigue (Meltzer and Mindell 2007).

When you review your trigger list, be sure to make note of how sleep deprivation impacts your yelling. Pay attention to the day after you've stayed up late watching a movie or caring for a sick child. What are you like the next day after waiting up until your teenager gets home from a party? If you have a new baby and an older child, you may find that nighttime feedings really set you up for early morning yelling as you try to get your older child out the door for school.

Fathers are also at risk for temper outbursts when they're not sleeping enough. Most couples with young children share the burden of getting up at night to comfort a crying baby and waking up early with a child who pops up from sleep with the sunrise and roosters. If you're a single parent or your partner isn't around much to help, you need to be creative to find ways to catch up on your sleep. It might mean asking someone to take your child to their house for a few hours so you can get a good nap or taking a sick day from work to have a day in bed.

Getting more sleep is really the only cure for sleep deprivation, although how to get more sleep is the challenge. There are many good books and websites about helping your child sleep through the night. I've listed some in the resources section.

Many parents I consult with tell me that even though their kids get to sleep on time and sleep soundly, the parents are still getting to bed late because of work demands. Some fire up the computer after their child is asleep and work for a few more hours before hitting the sack. Others stay up so they can have a little time with their spouse or partner; still others stay up late to clean the house and prepare for the next day.

I don't have any easy answers for you about how to get seven or eight hours of sleep each day, but I do think it's important. There were times when my kids spent the night at a friend's house, and instead of doing something fun, my husband and I went to bed early.

Evaluate and prioritize what you do each week, and get more sleep. You will be more likely to solve problems in a calm and reasonable way without yelling when you've had a good night's sleep.

No Time for Yourself

Do the words "I take care of everyone else but me!" sound familiar? A top complaint I hear from parents is the lack of alone time to refuel. One father said, "I can't believe how much I miss the simple things like going to the ball game with the guys, having time to read a novel, or taking a long shower." When your tank is on empty, you're more likely to become irritable and impatient.

• Lisa's Story

Lisa, a parent of two-year-old twins, decided not to go back to work once her maternity leave was over. She wanted to take care of her children, especially since her son had special needs. Her job as a project manager had been demanding.

Lisa felt that occasional child care was a luxury she couldn't afford since she no longer contributed to the household income. She was exhausted, overwhelmed, and lonely. She missed the positive feedback and adult conversation she used to get from her coworkers and clients.

After a few weeks at home, Lisa noticed she was yelling at her twins more and more but felt too ashamed to tell anyone how bad she felt. She had no time to herself, except for a few hours after the kids were in bed, and then she was cleaning up and doing her best to fit in a little time with her partner. Many nights, Lisa stayed up late to check her e-mail and keep up with friends online, which added to her sleep deprivation.

One day her sister came over to help because Lisa was sick. Lisa burst into tears and cried more than she had in a long time. She realized that she had lost her sense of who she was and felt hopeless about her life. She was desperate for time alone, time when she could turn her mother-brain off.

It's not unusual for moms to be too embarrassed to ask for help, especially when they compare themselves to mothers who work full time and have to take care of the house and kids in the evenings. Lisa had the false impression that she needed to give "all of herself" to the kids. Her yelling diminished greatly after she signed the twins up for child care two mornings a week. She even started doing a little consulting to bring in enough money to balance the budget. She talked to other mothers of twins and decided to be honest about her need to have some time away from her children.

Lisa's situation is challenging, but she is fortunate—she has resources and people to help her out. For some, the challenge is in not having the financial resources to get the help they need. What happens when there isn't any money for child care or when a parent has to go to a demanding job, even if she wants to stay home with the baby? What if you don't have any relatives nearby to help you or you're living in a neighborhood where you don't feel safe? Maybe you're a parent making ends meet with the help of unemployment and doing your best to raise your children even though you're worried every day. How do you find time to relax or rest? One key is to find or develop a community of like-minded parents. I had regular weekly exchanges with friends when my children were young. It's a wonderful way to have no-cost child care and build meaningful relationships. Local parenting resource agencies often have drop-in playgroups so you can get to know other parents. Asking for help is a valuable skill to develop, and other parents may crave your company and help as well.

No matter what your circumstances, your children will be better off if you can be more present with them and yell less. It's something you can do, and this book will help you learn how.

Dads Get Tired and Irritable Too

A few decades ago, it was generally more common for women to do the bulk of the child rearing, while fathers were thought to be breadwinners. Today, as fathers continue to take more and more of an active role in raising kids, cooking, shopping, and cleaning house, they too may suffer from having little time to refuel and rest from these labors. From single dads, to gay dads, to foster dads, to stepdads, to married dads, to grandfathers, men are more and more involved in the lives of their children—and more likely to be exhausted by that effort.

When I talk to dads, I hear how much they love their kids and how worn down they often feel. Like moms, dads are trying to do it all and finding that the internal and external expectations are high. A major complaint is the lack of downtime, whether it is alone, with a spouse or partner, or with friends. Without downtime or some way to refuel, men too become more irritable.

Zak is doing his best to be there for his four kids. His wife works, and she has also decided to go back to school. Zak works the night shift as a nurse and takes care of their kids in the morning before school and when they come home in the afternoon. He gets about six hours of sleep on a good day. His life consists of sleeping, shopping, cooking, working, and caring for the kids.

He and his wife have little time together, and he has no time for any of his hobbies, like playing the guitar in the band he started with his friends. Because his fuel tank is empty and he's sleep deprived, he yells a lot at the kids. He expects them to be more mature than their age, and he gets annoyed when they play loudly in the house.

Zak realized he needed help one day when the kids were playing hide-and-seek in the house while he was trying to rest. When his son opened the bedroom door to look for his sister, Zak lost it. He was woken up from a deep sleep and screamed, "I'm trying to sleep, and you don't even give a %#*@(#. How many times do I have to tell you not to interrupt me when I'm resting? You only care about yourself. Now get out of here and don't let me hear you till dinner." His intensity increased as he yelled, "I wish I could live by myself so I could just get some sleep!" Immediately, he regretted his words, but there was no taking them back.

Zak thought of himself as a loving dad, so when he heard himself rage at his son, he felt terrible. He apologized and told his son that he was sorry for yelling and for saying mean things. Zak realized that his life had gotten out of control and that he and his wife would have to do some serious thinking about their priorities.

You may recognize that kind of outburst. Good people can easily lose it with their kids when stress builds and their internal and external resources diminish.

Learning About Yourself

Most parents tell me that as they begin to observe their own yelling behavior and learn more about their triggers and escalating thoughts and feelings, they almost automatically begin to yell less. As you begin to spend more time observing yourself with your child, you will find that you respond differently to your child's misbehavior.

Having a firm intention to yell less and identifying your triggers are key to changing your yelling behavior. But don't stop with that. If you want to sustain a calmer and more patient approach in response to your child's behaviors and needs, there is more to learn, think about, and do. Sarah, a participant in my class and the mother of a three-year-old, told me, "I feel like what I'm learning in this class, and from my reflections, is that it is really all about cultivating inner peace and serenity. That it's about me, not anything my kids do."

We will get back to your child's behavior in future chapters. Right now, however, let's take some time to find ways to increase your awareness of your own thoughts, feelings, and actions.

Observing Yourself

Self-observation is an invitation to become familiar with your thoughts, feelings, and actions, without judgment. It's an important and useful habit to cultivate and one that is fundamental to yelling less.

The concept of self-observation was not a value passed on to me as a child or young adult from my parents or teachers. I don't remember anyone talking about paying attention to how I was feeling or even being interested in what I was thinking. My parents loved me, but I received the consistent message that I needed to be different than I was to satisfy the adults around me. What I felt rarely seemed important to others.

Self-acceptance, mindfulness, and self-awareness were not subjects taught in school or practiced by anyone I knew. It wasn't until I had two young children and my first marriage was failing (in the 1970s) that I stumbled upon Eastern teachings that encouraged me to take an honest look at myself and the people around me. I was going through a difficult time and had a deep desire to understand more about my life, my past hurts, my strengths, and how to be present for my kids. I wanted to learn as much as I could. But I quickly came to see that self-observation is not an easy thing to remember to do!

When you observe yourself, you become aware of your habitual behavior and the nonstop chatter in your head. For example, if you always carry a purse or a briefcase in your right hand, try for a day to carry it in your left hand. You'll come to see how automatically it winds up in your right hand and how frequently you forget your intention. Thoughts of the past or future run through our minds all the time— just try counting from one to one hundred without thinking of something else. We spend a great deal of energy away from the present moment, where life is taking place.

Remembering to observe yourself moment by moment takes practice. After almost forty years of practice I still forget, but more often than not I'm able to observe what's going on around me without just thinking about what has passed and what is to come. I learned not to focus on the times when I forget to observe myself but instead to be grateful for the times when I remember.

You will see that it's easy to forget, but over time your ability to come back to the present moment without judgment increases. You might want to set an alarm on your phone to help you come back to the moment. When you hear the alarm, you can pay attention to your breath and bodily sensations. Check in with yourself to see how you are feeling. A good way to observe yourself, as you do the many tasks you need to do each day, is to put your attention on your arms and legs and your breathing. So if you're doing the dishes, you can follow your breath, sense your hands in the water, and feel your feet on the ground. This practice will help you stay more aware of what's going on and be less reactive to the next interruption or stressful situation.

Practicing Mindfulness

The Mindfulness-Based Stress Reduction Program was developed by Jon Kabat-Zinn (1990) at the University of Massachusetts Medical Center. I learned about his work when I was a nurse at Kaiser Permanente in the 1990s. I was impressed by the concept that learning to be mindful could have a dramatic impact on a person's physical and mental health.

Mindfulness concepts and exercises were then being taught to patients with chronic illnesses. They learned how to change their attitude toward their pain, to be patient and nonjudging, to be kind to themselves, and to be more accepting about their health. In his book, *Full Catastrophe Living*, Kabat-Zinn (1990, 2) defines mindfulness as "moment-to-moment awareness, cultivated by purposefully paying attention to things we ordinarily never give a moment's thought to."

Breathing is an example of something we usually don't pay attention to. Under unusual circumstances, you will notice your breath—when you hike up a hill; run a marathon; or become ill, anxious, or afraid. Noticing your breathing is a way to come back to the present moment. Try to notice what your breathing is like when you are yelling, if you can remember to do so.

You can start being mindful today. It doesn't take much time, because you can focus your attention on observing yourself as you do your daily tasks. Begin to pay attention to yourself when you are driving your car, brushing your teeth, or drinking coffee. When you feel impatient at a traffic light, take a few minutes to sense your body and your breathing. Notice your hands: Are they clutching the steering wheel? Look at the trees or buildings around you. Is your mind in the past, future, or present?

This moment, right now, is the time when you can be fully present. When your child is having a tantrum, take that moment to see if you can become aware of your breathing and body sensations as well.

Observing Without Judgment or Criticism

If you already practice mindfulness, meditation, or self-observation, you can use your skills as they relate to your child's behavior and your response. The idea is *not* to judge or criticize yourself as being right or wrong. Your task is to discover and examine the truth about yourself, so that you have more choice.

There is a relief that can come when you see the truth about how you move in the world. If you can be kind to yourself when you see things you don't like, you will be more willing to keep looking. For example, you may notice how you get impatient and speak in an annoyed tone of voice when your child says he has to go to the bathroom, right when it's time to leave the house for school. Perhaps you notice how impatience often precedes your yelling. If you pay attention to your impatience, you will learn how often it happens. With observation and compassion you get a better picture of what you are like and how being on time is a huge issue for you.

Noticing your thoughts, feelings, and physical response to stress—without criticizing yourself—is crucial. There's no need to be hard on yourself. We all long to be accepted for who we are, even when we make mistakes.

EXERCISE: Your Body Reveals Your Thoughts and Feelings

When you're busy getting ready for work or making breakfast, you're probably not paying attention to how your body feels. If you were to bring your attention to your body, you would notice changes taking place when your child slows you down or irritates you. Eventually, becoming familiar with your physical changes will help you realize you are angry or frustrated and give you the signal to do something before the negative feelings take over.

For example, when I felt angry because my children wouldn't stop bothering each other, my breathing got faster, I started to pace, and I felt tension in my neck, jaw, and hands. These were warning signals for me that I learned to pay attention to over time.

Your Self-Inventory

Check off the physical changes you notice before you start to yell.

☐ *Your hands get tense, and you make a fist.*

☐ *Your body temperature rises.*

☐ *Your voice gets louder.*

☐ *Your teeth clench and your jaw tightens.*

☐ *Your breathing is faster and more in your chest than in your belly.*

☐ *Your heart beats faster.*

☐ *Your head or neck feels tense.*

☐ *Your blood pressure feels like it's going up.*

☐ *You squint, and you make a funny face.*

☐ *Your hands are placed on your hips, or you start to point.*

☐ *Your feet are tapping, or you start to pace.*

☐ *Your face gets red and hot.*

☐ _____

The next time you start to yell, see if you can sense your physical responses. This is a key step in being able to stop your yelling reaction before it takes over. When I was learning to pay attention to my physical reactions, I used to ask myself questions like, *What's my posture like right now, and what gestures am I making? How about my facial expressions, breathing, and tone of voice?* It takes practice to become familiar with the physical changes you experience.

Try This Now

Remind yourself right now to sense your arms and legs. How do they feel? Heavy, light, achy, cramped? Now notice your breathing. Without stressing, take a few easy breaths. When you're ready, begin to pay attention to the sounds around you, to the quality of the light, to the shapes you see as you look away from the page. What's different for you?

From this calmer state, you will automatically notice more. Do this when you're with your kids, and you will be more responsive to them and less likely to yell.

What Do Your Children See?

Whether or not you are aware of yourself, your children are constantly observing you. What do you think they see on your face or in your body when you're annoyed or angry? You might be surprised.

John, a psychologist and great dad, told me the story of how his nine-year-old daughter Kerry gave him feedback about the "morning monster." One day at breakfast, Kerry walked into the kitchen making a mean face and jumping around with a wide stance, making apelike monster sounds. John laughed and asked her what she was doing and what kind of animal she was. She replied, "I'm being the daddy monster. This is what you look like in the morning."

Chagrined, John asked her why she thought he looked like this, and she simply said, "Cause you're angry all the time in the morning." John thanked her for letting him know, and he sheepishly walked off and looked in the mirror to see if the monster was still there. It was.

John realized he was rushing around in the morning with a million things on his mind, and although he wasn't always angry, he was preoccupied and frequently irritated by how long things were taking and how much there was to do. His daughter's feedback increased his desire to observe himself and be more present with what was going on in the moment, rather than just worrying about the future.

Your children are perceptive and sensitive, and you can be too. Now it's your turn to see yourself. When you get a glimpse of your angry monster, see if you can become friends and get to know each other.

Preparing for Fight or Flight

You may have heard of the fight-or-flight response. Walter Bradford Cannon first described this in the early 1900s. He researched how animals react to threats and the role of the sympathetic nervous system as an animal prepares for fight or flight. He studied the impact of stress on the internal organs of animals when he did autopsies and saw the damage done (Cannon 1915).

Our sympathetic nervous systems also work to mobilize the body's fight-or-flight response. When your sympathetic nervous system is called into action, stress hormones such as epinephrine, norepinephrine, and cortisol cause many physiological changes. For example, your blood pressure increases, your heart beats faster, and your digestion slows down. In the face of a threat, such as a person trying to break into your house, these changes help your body and mind prepare to fight or run away.

When stress hormones are "turned on" a good deal of the time, your body suffers, leading to an array of health challenges and diseases. Cannon's work was the beginning of the extensive research that continues today as scientists and health practitioners learn more about the consequences of the fight or flight response and anger in humans.

The Fight or Flight Response in Everyday Practice

Stress may also cause you to overreact and see threats that don't really exist. You may find yourself scanning the environment for the enemy at 9 a.m. when you're trying to get out of the house with a baby and a three-year-old. There is no enemy, but you're on hyperalert and ready to fight your toddler if he doesn't behave. When you are surprised or startled by your child's actions, can't find your keys, trip over the toys that should have been put away, your body thinks it's either under attack or needs to be on the attack.

Of course, the fight or flight response doesn't end when your child gets older. Yoko's story is one that most parents of teens will relate to.

• Yoko's Story

Yoko's sixteen-year-old son, Kai, invited a bunch of friends over one night, without asking his mom's permission. Yoko went out on a date, and Kai assumed she would be home late. Unfortunately for Kai, Yoko felt sick and returned home early. She walked in the door and heard music blasting. The lights were low, and a couple of teenagers were making out on the couch. Kai and a bunch of his friends were smoking and drinking in the backyard.

In an instant Yoko felt angry and afraid. Her thoughts were: *How dare he have a party? What if the neighbors see him smoking? And there are girls here!*

She immediately began to yell and say things like, "What are you all doing here? I'm going to call the cops if you don't leave this minute! You're not old enough to drink!" Without talking to Kai, she assumed the worst about his friends. She kept mumbling and pacing until everyone was gone, and then shouted at Kai, "You're grounded for a long time! I can't trust you with anything." Kai cursed his mother under his breath and slammed his bedroom door.

If Yoko had taken some deep breaths, stopped the escalating thoughts in her head, found her son, and took him aside, her intensity would have been reduced. She needed to clear her head before responding to a challenging but not unheard-of teen mistake. And, it would have worked out better if she had taken time to cool off before handing out any punishment. She humiliated her son in front of his friends, and as a result their relationship suffered.

There Is Nothing Wrong with Feeling Angry

It's important to remember that *there is nothing wrong with feeling angry*. Yoko had every right to feel angry about Kai's behavior. Chances are you would have been angry too if you came home to a renegade teen party. It was Yoko's response to the situation—her escalating thoughts and feelings and her reactive anger—that caused her to do and say hurtful things.

You might think that her son's behavior was the cause of her reaction, and if he hadn't had the party, none of it would have happened. It's true that Kai's actions plus Yoko's thoughts triggered her yelling, but your child's actions are not an excuse to lose it, threaten, scream, and humiliate him or her. If you've done something similar, you're not alone. This kind of reaction happens all the time, but the goal you have identified for yourself is to learn to be responsive rather than overreact. An appropriate response might have been to get Kai to ask his guests to clean up and then leave, and then for Yoko to tell Kai that she is disappointed and angry and will talk with him about consequences once she has calmed down.

I know from experience that it's worth learning how to manage anger. In circumstances when I was present enough to stay calm I was able to say to my child, "I'm too angry to talk to you right now. We'll talk when I've cooled off. Please go to your room and think about what just happened." It takes much more time and emotional effort to repair a relationship that has suffered from angry words and yelling than to give yourself some time to cool off.

In future chapters we'll go into the details of tracking your yelling triggers and making plans for doing something different. For now, simply focus on becoming familiar with yourself. If you would like to learn more about self-observation or mindfulness practices, you'll find information in the resource section. In chapters 3 and 4 we will dig a little deeper into the reasons you yell. Your understanding and insight are the foundation for finding solutions that are in line with your individual situation and values.

A Thought to Consider: *My feelings and thoughts don't have to rule me.*

Feelings and thoughts come and go throughout the day. Get to know their patterns and their rhythms, and understand that you don't have to be at their mercy.

Learn to divide your attention. Put some attention on what's going on with your child and some on what's happening in your mind and body. And if you need an extra boost to be more aware of yourself, get a little more sleep.

Chapter 3

"Why Am I *Really* Yelling?"

Digging Deeper

"I know I shouldn't yell at my daughter when she makes a mess feeding herself, but the anger just wells up inside of me. She is adorable and funny, but I feel overwhelmed and irritable most days. I continually doubt my ability to be a good father, especially when I hear the words that come out of my mouth when I yell."

—James, father of two-year-old Sasha and six-year-old Trevor

Sudden yelling or intense feelings of anger that seem to come out of nowhere may not make any sense to you. A child's mealtime mess may appear to be the trigger that sets you off yelling, but there may be something more to your strong reaction. Sometimes when you dig, you can find what would otherwise be hidden.

The efforts you make to look beyond the everyday triggers of yelling will help you create a more harmonious household and a closer bond with your children. If that sounds good to you, get out your shovel and start digging.

Generations of Yellers

Yelling may be a part of your family culture, passed down from previous generations. When you were little, your parents were your first teachers, and you learned about the world by watching them. If you had parents who frequently yelled, it might feel natural for you to yell at your children. On the other hand, you may work hard to stay calm, but under stress, yelling might be your default setting because of your childhood experiences. Young children love their parents and look to them for guidance, even when parents yell or punish harshly.

Unlearning Bad Behavior

There are good things your parents did when you were growing up that you will try to emulate and other things you will work hard not to repeat. Perhaps you have fond memories of planting vegetables in the garden with your dad. You learned skills that you have used as an adult, and the time alone with your dad was precious. At the same time, you have promised yourself not to curse at your kids when they make mistakes, like your dad did.

Your dad taught you how easy it is for parents to lose their temper, and now you're working to unlearn what he taught you. Don't be surprised if you find it challenging to remember what it was like for you as a child. Find a quiet place, sit comfortably, and remember what you can. If you allow yourself some time and space, you'll have memories to work with that will help you break the cycle of yelling. When you gently bring past experiences into the present, you can expand the possibilities, and be less reactive and impulsive and more thoughtful and calm in response to your child's behavior.

• James's Story

James grew up in a military family that moved frequently, with parents who disciplined their children by yelling and spanking. His parents yelled hurtful words at the kids and at each other on a regular basis. They were strict parents and often got angry for reasons that James didn't understand.

James was particularly afraid of his father and learned at an early age to be sneaky and not to get caught. One time, when he broke his mother's favorite holiday platter, he accused his little brother of dropping it, just to avoid his father's wrath. As the oldest child, his instinct was to protect his siblings, but he learned to blame them for his mistakes to avoid being the target of his parents' anger.

James's parents valued saving money, working hard, getting a good education, and keeping their house and kids neat and clean. James was told he couldn't have his friends over to play because they made too much of a mess. His parents were private people, and laughter and fun were not part of his daily experience at home. He had to do well at school, and if his homework wasn't up to par, yelling and punishment followed. One night, when his father was shouting at him for not getting his science project done, James vowed to never yell at his kids.

As an adult, James works hard as a high school teacher and is well liked by his students and coworkers. He loves his work but is stressed out by financial challenges. He and his partner, Chris, are hoping to buy a house so they can put down roots. For now they have to rent a place that's too small but in a good neighborhood for the kids. James is determined to provide stability for his kids, something he didn't have growing up.

Years of conditioning are hard to shake, and James gets discouraged when he observes how quickly he starts yelling at his daughter. Despite his insight and sensitivity, more often than not, he can't seem to stop himself from yelling. His son, Trevor, is mild-mannered and easy to discipline. His daughter, Sasha, is strong willed, intense, and wants to do everything by herself. (In chapter 4 we will discuss the role that temperament plays in triggering yelling.) Sasha's strong nature sets James off, especially when she cries or has a tantrum when she doesn't get her way. When James was young, crying would have meant more yelling from his parents. He had to learn to be quiet and tough. Angry feelings just weren't allowed for kids.

As you reflect on your childhood experiences, motivations for your yelling may come to light. I find that new things occur to me on a regular basis about how my childhood still influences my relationships with my adult children. I still hear my mother's voice when I ask my twenty-five-year-old daughter if she is warm enough as she leaves the house. I can also picture my father questioning me about everything I did, as I see the annoyed look on my son's face when I ask one too many questions.

"How Can I Stop Being Like My Dad?"

James is in a situation that many parents find themselves in. When he comes to the parenting class I teach, he says, with tears in his eyes, "I don't want to yell like my parents did. I'm great with my students, but I turn into a mean guy with my daughter. Please help me stop being like my dad."

During the class parents reflect on their yelling triggers to see if there are correlations to their own childhood experiences. After listening to other parents, James begins to understand on a deeper level that how his parents treated him influences how he deals with his kids. James knew that he had been acting like his dad some of the time. He said that he could hear it in his voice, and feel it in his body whenever his hands began to fold in front of him as he became irritated and stiff. As he digs more, he realizes that his parents' insistence on keeping the house clean all the time plays a role in his reaction to Sasha's messy eating. When he was young, playing with food was not allowed.

Becoming aware of your gestures, posture, facial expressions, and tone of voice can help you be more aware of your actions and sometimes the thoughts and emotions connected to them. When you're motivated to change, tuning in to your body will give you clues to how you're feeling and what you need.

James had never connected the dots before in regard to his parents' rules around neatness and his discomfort when his daughter made messes. When you see a connection like that, you move closer to having a choice about how you will respond next time. The insight is like a light going on to help you see your way toward a parenting style that's your own, not just a reaction to your parents' style.

Is There a Yelling Legacy in Your Family?

"I definitely fall into the 'generations of yellers' category. Once I left home and got away from my parents' yelling, I didn't think about yelling as an issue until my first son was about two years old.

I really wish that books like What to Expect When You're Expecting *had a chapter about preparing for a child by reflecting on your own childhood. I wish that someone would have warned me that this yelling demon would rear its head."*

—Jess, the mother of two active boys

Your parents may not have been able to break the cycle of frequent yelling that was passed on to them, but you can.

Now, begin to reflect on the following questions. Your answers will help you understand how your reactions have been shaped by your environment. You can then use these reflections about your yelling heritage to create new traditions that will help you become the kind of parent you wish to be.

- Did your parents, grandparents, or guardians frequently yell at you or your siblings?

- How often did they yell?

- What kinds of behaviors did they yell about?

- When they yelled, did they say hurtful things?

- Did the yelling precede physical or verbal abuse?

- How did you feel when you were yelled at? Some possibilities are afraid, humiliated, angry, relieved, numb, betrayed, or rejected.

- Did you think you were a "bad child"?

- Did you think you deserved to be yelled at?

- Did they ever apologize?

- What methods of discipline did your parents use that you appreciated, if any?

- What do you wish they'd done instead of yelling?

- How did their yelling affect the way you discipline your child?

- How did their yelling affect the way you feel about yourself as an adult?

Consider reviewing your answers with your parenting partner or a good friend. Find out about her experiences of parental yelling. Your efforts will help you heal, as well as break the cycle of yelling. If you prefer, write your answers in a journal. Writing them down will help you remember and highlight the areas you want to pay particular attention to.

The Opportunity for Change

We have all had difficult experiences in childhood, and we coped as well as we could. As an adult, you have the capacity to face your childhood experiences, understand a multitude of feelings, and change your patterns and behaviors. You can learn a great deal by looking back with compassion at the child you were, and the challenges you and your parents faced.

When I think about some hurtful times of my childhood, I feel grateful that I've been able to surpass my parents in understanding myself and understanding the needs of my children. My parents did the best they could, considering what they knew and their life circumstances. I have forgiven them for their mistakes, although I haven't forgotten.

I also feel remorse for causing my children pain because of my blind spots, immaturity, and inexperience when they were young. It's normal to have feelings of remorse when you become aware of your mistakes. It's also a huge relief to take an honest look at the imperfect condition we all find ourselves in as parents. Remember, you're not alone in this journey.

Displaced Anger: Whom Am I Really Angry At?

Our children are sometimes convenient targets for the anger we feel in reaction to other people. Displaced anger can occur when you direct your anger at someone other than the person you originally felt angry toward. Often people choose someone who is safer, like a child, as a target for their anger.

After you yell, ask yourself, *Whom am I really angry at?* You might find it's not your child at all, but someone else: your boss, spouse, partner, or mother.

James, for example, is yelling about the mess his daughter is making, but it is not only a reaction to his restrictive childhood. As he considers the question, he realizes that he's also angry with his partner, Chris. James does the morning and evening routine with both kids when Chris is away on business trips. When James is on duty 24/7 and has too much to get done, his anger toward Chris gets ignited. James's anger is a clue that he needs to come to terms with the parenting load he is carrying and to communicate better with Chris. Figuring out what he needs from Chris will help to defuse the anger and frustration he feels and expresses when he yells at the kids.

Think about a time when you yelled at your kids because you were really angry with someone else. Here are a few more examples to help you see if you displace your anger toward someone else onto your kids.

• Tom's Story

Tom's supervisor is critical and insensitive. Almost every day, Tom comes home from work feeling angry and resentful. One evening, after a hard day and a long drive home, he walked into the house to discover that his son hadn't done his chores. Without much thought, Tom began to yell, "Why didn't you clean your room yet? I told you to do it yesterday. You're lazy! You always wait till the last minute to get anything done!"

If Tom would stop and listen to himself, he might realize that he sounds a lot like his boss. Just a few hours ago, his supervisor said, "Tom, I'm disappointed in you for not completing the report today. I hope you'll get a better system for managing your schedule. Your job depends on it." Tom felt threatened by his boss. Driving home, his escalating thoughts took over—*I'm a screwup! I'll never get a raise at this rate*—and continued in a shame-filled loop.

When he came home feeling afraid and angry and when he saw that his son had put off his chores, he yelled and said unkind things. His son's messy room, plus thoughts of his son's laziness, set off the yelling. He was discharging the discomfort he was feeling and may also have been reacting to things he saw in his son that he didn't like about himself.

Sometimes you can catch displaced anger before you yell by seeing that you're beginning to overreact to something that normally wouldn't cause you to yell. Here's another example of displaced anger, this time from my personal experience.

• Rona's Story

One evening, years ago, I lost it and yelled at my kids because they weren't cooperating with me to get the table set. It had been a rushed afternoon, and I had a meeting I needed to attend that evening. My husband, Mick, was relaxing, engrossed in the newspaper, not aware of what was going on around him.

In hindsight, I realized that I was yelling at the kids mostly for Mick's sake. I was mad that he could relax and ignore what was going on, while I scurried around getting things done and becoming more and more annoyed. My intense reaction was out of proportion. A child not wanting to stop playing to set the table isn't a huge offense. Normally, the kids just needed a reminder.

My yelling at the kids had the desired effect: It jarred Mick out of his newspaper trance. He heard that I needed help. But I wasn't straightforward enough to ask for help, and I resented that Mick didn't check in to see what was needed without me asking. Sound familiar? I can even remember my escalating thoughts. They went something like this: *Why is he always so oblivious? He gets to read while I have to do everything. And why can't the kids just do what I ask them to? Everyone gets to do what they want except me.*

In reality, Mick did his share around the house, so I was able to see that my stress was causing me to feel resentful. I was sorry that I had dumped that on my kids. When Mick heard me yelling at the kids, he came to my rescue. He could have chimed in and yelled at the kids as well, but he maintained a calm emotional state rather than matching mine.

Can you see how this scenario could encourage me to continue to yell at my kids? Mick got up from reading and relaxing, took charge, and got the kids to set the table. My yelling, ironically, had gotten me what I wanted. This dynamic could have kept me from learning to communicate with the kids respectfully and with my husband directly, instead of through the kids. Yelling at my children to set the table was unnecessary. Underlying my angry feelings toward my family were my feelings of disconnection from myself and my thoughts about what I needed. Once you begin to notice that you sometimes displace your anger or frustration and yell at your kids to discharge your feelings toward someone else, change will begin: you will yell less.

Learning from Your Anger

Anger is probably unavoidable. But becoming aware of your anger—whom or what you are really angry at and how you choose to express it—can actually help you stop yelling.

When I became angry with my kids instead of my husband, for example, my anger helped me see that I wasn't paying attention to what I needed. I certainly wasn't asking my husband for help before I lost my senses. But because I was disconnected from my emotions and needs, I didn't notice how I was feeling until *after* I yelled at the kids and my husband took over. I felt lousy about myself after I yelled, and I didn't want to do that anymore. With that, my resolve to change increased.

Your anger can be defused or ignited. It's your choice, once you understand your goals and learn new skills. You can find a practical and thoughtful exploration of anger in the book *When Anger Hurts* (McKay, Rogers, and McKay 2003). I refer to this book because I found it so helpful in working with parents who had never learned about anger management or the concepts of cognitive behavioral therapy. In the book, McKay talks about how anger can sometimes help us by serves as a warning sign that there is a problem that needs to be dealt with.

For example, if you find yourself getting angry and yelling whenever your teenager leaves her dishes in the sink, some action is needed. You might call a family meeting to reiterate the rules and review the consequences for ignoring them. (We will discuss ways to express anger without yelling or saying hurtful words in part 2.)

When Yelling and Anger Lead to Abuse

Feeling angry is different than using your anger as a weapon to hurt or attack someone else. Everyone experiences feelings of anger, but what you do with your feelings is vital to your relationships and to your own well-being.

There is extensive evidence that "letting off steam" is not good for you or for the people you care about. As the authors of *When Anger Hurts* explain, "Expressing anger tends to make you even angrier and solidifies an angry attitude" (McKay, Rodgers, and McKay 2003, 18).

Anger can quickly lead to rage, a loss of control that can lead to shouting, becoming violent (throwing or breaking things or physically hurting someone), or other bullying behaviors. If your anger is escalating and getting difficult for you to manage, you could become abusive toward your children.

In a *20/20* TV segment that I was involved with as an advisor, they put cameras in the homes of three families in which parents wanted to reduce their anger toward their children. One mother, who was often loving and playful with her children, became both verbally and physically abusive when she was under excessive stress. She was pregnant with her third child, and she had been raised by parents who yelled all of the time. In the video, we see her yelling at her son to eat his food on the floor like the dog, because he isn't listening to her.

On another day the crying and whining of her kids really gets to her. Her yelling escalates, and she suddenly picks up her son and shakes him. Afterward she expresses profuse shame and guilt for her behavior and says, "I think they would be better off without me." This is an example of a mother who needs counseling and support for her anger and possible depression. It is clear that she cares deeply for her boys, but her stress is sky-high and she can't handle certain aspects of her day-to-day life.

Children love their parents, even if yelling or rage occurs. Your children need you to get support and help so you will honor them, not hurt them. Assess your expression of anger honestly. If your yelling turns to rage, professional help would be an important adjunct to what you are learning by reading this book.

Find the Feelings Beneath Your Anger

When you feel angry, you often experience other emotions that cause you stress. An angry yell can keep you from experiencing your other feelings, such as fear, grief, helplessness, or hurt. Yelling may help you release your stress or pain momentarily, but that reaction comes with consequences to you and your kids. If you want to understand yourself better, your anger can help point you in the direction of other feelings so you can experience them and do what's needed to take care of yourself.

The next time you yell at your child, ask yourself: *What do I feel right now besides anger? Are there other emotions more difficult to name?* Some examples are fear, sadness, grief, disappointment, rejection, hurt, shame, and frustration. When our go-to emotion is anger, we rarely get a chance to explore our emotional complexity.

James, who yelled at his daughter for making a mess, later reported an underlying feeling of sadness. He grieves not having had a childhood where he was free to be a kid, messes and all. As he reflects on what he didn't get as a child, he finds that he is more able to let his daughter have fun. It's a big accomplishment for him when he joins in with her and gets silly. His underlying sadness was keeping him from having fun with his daughter. He was trying to avoid painful memories but comes to see that naming them helps to reduce their power. He and his partner spend time talking about this together. Chris agrees to be more supportive and try to travel less in the coming year.

When I yelled at my kids for not setting the table, I had underlying feelings toward my husband that I was unaware of. It was easy to see that I was angry with him for not noticing I needed help. What was hard to admit was the hurt and disappointment I was also feeling because we hadn't spent any time alone together for weeks. We had missed our date night the week before, and it didn't seem like it mattered to him. When we talked about what happened that night after I yelled at the kids, I was able to tell him of my other feelings. He reassured me that he too missed having a night out together and insisted we put a new date on the calendar right away. This was not an unfamiliar pattern for us, and eventually, we were able to acknowledge our underlying feelings faster. I also worked on asking for help directly.

Healing can take place when you are able to see where you get stuck and recognize your feelings and needs. Ideally, you will work to become more like the parent you wish to be. The tools you are learning in this book will help you reduce your stress without yelling, recognize your feelings, and prepare you for situations that routinely trigger your yelling.

How's Your Health?

Your physical health affects your emotions, and your emotions affect your physical health. A large body of research shows that stress makes people more susceptible to illness, and many parents have high levels of stress, don't get enough sleep, eat on the run, and don't have time for exercise (Cohen et al. 1991, 1998). These are all lifestyle issues that can increase your chance of becoming ill and add to your irritability and yelling.

Many parents and guardians forget to pay attention to their own health. Ask yourself if you've been neglecting your health and reflect on your lifestyle. Have a serious talk with a loved one about how you can make small changes to reduce your stress and focus on your health. The following stories show how health issues can lead to yelling.

• José's Story

José has been having headaches but doesn't want to spend the money or time to get checked out by his doctor. He yells at his kids at the drop of a hat and is especially triggered when they are running around the house making noise, as kids do. He notices that right after he yells his headache gets worse, and he often gets flushed and a bit lightheaded. He's starting to worry that his blood pressure is going up, since hypertension and obesity run in his family.

José is in a cycle of discomfort, stress, yelling, and increased discomfort. His ongoing yelling is damaging to his health and the well-being of his kids. Like many men, Jose doesn't think it's necessary to go running to the doctor every time there is a little problem. He also doesn't want to hear about his poor eating habits and lack of exercise, which he is sure his doctor will bring up.

José is not alone in his pain. Extensive research done on men's health shows that they make far fewer visits to health professionals than women do. This pattern is prevalent regardless of a person's finances or ethnicity (Verbrugge 1985, 1989; Courtenay 2011).

Do you know a man who thinks he's invincible? Boys are often raised to be tough and risk takers. Our society and the media often perpetuate the image of the "stronger sex" not needing the help of others. Men's health expert and psychologist Will Courtenay (2011) says that most men are less likely to take responsibility for their health and well-being and in fact are not as knowledgeable as women, when it comes to issues of weight and health. He also reports that men tend to make false assumptions that they are less vulnerable to getting injured or sick.

You may not be like José, but I mention this here so you can think about your health needs. If your co-parent is a guy, find out when he had his last checkup. Try to encourage him (without nagging) to go to the doctor.

Grandma Hazel's Story

Hazel is a grandmother caring for four children, ages two to ten. Ever since she was given custody of her grandchildren, she and her husband have had little time to focus on their own health and well-being. I would often see Hazel when she brought the children to the pediatric office for their checkups or when they were ill. The oldest child had school problems, and Hazel was overwhelmed with trying to get her the help she needed. Hazel always brought the youngest one with her to all of the appointments so her husband could have a break at home. Frequently we could hear Hazel yelling at the toddler, "Now sit down and don't you dare touch anything here in the office. Just sit down and be quiet." When Hazel got distracted, the toddler would run down the hall laughing. Grandma Hazel would chase after her, yelling the entire way.

One day Hazel got dizzy and lost her balance. We all came to her aid, sent her to the medical department, and watched the kids while she was cared for. The episode was diagnosed as a transient ischemic attack (TIA). This is often referred to as a mini-stroke, and it happens when there is loss of blood flow to the brain. A TIA is a serious warning sign of a possible stroke and should not be ignored!

Hazel was treated for her high blood pressure and other medical issues. Getting attention and medication reduced her yelling, especially after her doctor sent her to a mindfulness-based stress reduction class as a part of her care. She was able to get a social worker to help her find the educational services she needed for her oldest grandchild and a subsidized preschool for the two-year-old.

Hazel would do anything for her grandkids, but she needed to see that her health was a huge factor in her irritability, fatigue, and yelling. Her stress impacted her health, and her health issues increased her stress. There are increasing numbers of grandparents who are raising their grandchildren who don't have time to take good care of themselves in their golden years.

Shame

When I picked up Brené Brown's book *The Gifts of Imperfection* (2010, xi) at a weekend women's retreat, I couldn't put it down until I'd read the entire book. It helped me let go of another layer of self-criticism.

"How much we know and understand about ourselves is critically important," Brown writes, "but there is something that is even more essential to living a wholehearted life: loving ourselves" (xi).

When you feel ashamed, you're likely to have an underlying sense that you are bad, flawed, or unlovable. These shameful feelings can easily be transmitted to your children when you yell at them or say harsh words to point out their imperfections. If you are hard on yourself, you will also be hard on your kids. When your child does something you disapprove of, there is a big difference between yelling, "You're such a mean big brother. Why can't you ever be nice?" and saying, "When you don't let your brother have a turn with the ball, he feels sad." The first statement implies that the child is bad, and the second one points to the specific behavior you are hoping to correct and focuses on empathy. When you yell at children and call them names such as bad, mean, stupid, or selfish, you encourage shame in them and perpetuate the shame you feel underneath your yelling.

Healing Your Own Shame

As in most things related to parenting, starting with yourself is primary. In this case, healing your own shame is the first step.

The best way I know to heal shame is to acknowledge when shame is present. Get to know what that feels like in your body and mind.

When I have the experience of feeling ashamed, I usually feel small, foggy, and low energy. I can also recognize what's going on because my emotional reaction is out of proportion to the event that has just occurred. If I find myself feeling like a failure, ready to give up, wanting to suck my thumb and retreat into a fetal position, then I know shame has reared its ugly head. With shame I have tunnel vision, and the mistakes I've made are highlighted at the end of the tunnel for me to dwell on.

I've learned to ask myself why I feel so lousy and to share those feelings with a sympathetic listener. I know that talking to my husband (who will always listen) or a friend takes courage and helps break the spell of shame. Now when I sense feelings of shame or humiliation from my childhood, I observe them. I remind myself that I'm an adult now with much more freedom and power than I had when I was little. I have choices and a deep desire to treat myself with kindness and respect. When you don't hide from your feelings of shame, they have much less power.

Shame is a human emotion that all people feel, but don't talk about enough. If it stays hidden, it will come out in negative thoughts and actions. If you bring it to light, it will have the chance to dissipate. When you feel shame, call a friend or loved one and tell her you need to talk because you're in a moment of shame, and you want to come back to a place of compassion toward yourself.

If you were brought up with shame, notice if you are being overly critical and shaming of your children when things aren't as you wish they would be. This was true of Lin, a mother I met with to discuss the challenges she was having with her daughter. She was smart, attentive, and sincerely motivated to make changes in her parenting practices.

• Lin's Story

Lin, a forty-year-old graphic designer who has two young children, was raised in the United States by parents who were born in China. Her parents are loving grandparents and help out with the children. They care for the one-year-old all day and take the two-and-a-half-year-old to day care. Lin is ambivalent about their involvement because they are critical of her parenting. She appreciates and relies on their help but often goes to bed feeling like a failure as a mom.

Lin's parents complain that she yells at the kids too much, and at other times they tell her she spoils the kids by letting them get what they want when they cry. Lin is trying to figure out what parenting approach to take, but most days she's too exhausted to even think about it and tunes out in front of her computer when the kids are finally asleep. Her husband tries to help her, but they get into arguments instead of agreements.

One day her older child Mai, who was being potty trained, looked at Lin and with a smile said, "Look, Mommy,

I'm peeing on the floor." Lin quickly grabbed her and shouted, "Mai, that's disgusting. You're naughty, and you must clean it up right now before your baby brother slips in your smelly pee." Lin made her clean it up all by herself and then sent her to her room. Her escalating thought when her daughter peed on the floor was *She's doing this on purpose just to get my attention. She knows better.* In this instance Lin was unable to teach her child without shaming her.

Lin doesn't remember being potty trained when she was young, but her mother tells her that it was easy to do, and that Lin was a good girl and never had accidents. This just adds to Lin's feeling of incompetence. She's ashamed of her imperfections, even though she knows it's normal to make mistakes and not know what to do as a parent. And she also knows that it's normal for a child to have accidents and that shame does not help in the process. She feels remorse for not stopping the hurtful words that just come sailing out of her mouth. She has never really talked about the shame and lack of nurturing she experienced as a child.

Lin feels overwhelmed trying to balance her work and home life. She is a perfectionist and strives to live up to an image she has of a mother who can look good, be sexy, work hard, keep a clean house, and raise well-behaved children. She is unhappy in her marriage and knows that counseling would help. She is almost ready to take the leap and get help to bring intimacy and friendship back into her relationship with her husband. She can see how feeling close to him would reduce her yelling and bring more pleasure back into her life.

I see Lin as someone on the beginning of a journey toward health and healing. Her frequent yelling has opened her eyes to her anger, frustration, and shame. She wants to learn new ways to communicate with her family. Her awareness of her yelling has helped her get more in touch with what it was like for her as a little girl, when she was yelled at, punished, and humiliated. Her parents continue to make her feel bad, even now that she is an adult.

A Thought to Consider:
Why am I so angry?

It takes courage to dig deeper and uncover obstacles to respectful communication with your child. Do you come from a generation of yellers? Are you angry with someone else? Is your health impacting your mood? Do you have other feelings waiting to be noticed? These are all questions worth exploring.

If you feel like you don't have time to dig deeper, keep in mind that in the long run, it will save you time. Participating in power struggles and yelling matches takes time and energy and can take a toll on your health.

The next time you find yourself yelling at your kids, take that opportunity to increase your self-awareness: Dig deeper to discover what's hiding underneath your anger. Come face-to-face with your fear, bring loving kindness to your shame, or forgive yourself for the embarrassment you feel because you yelled in the grocery store. The feelings underneath your anger need recognition, attention, and compassion.

Chapter 4

"What's Temperament Got to Do with It?"

Adapting Your Parenting Style to Your Child's Temperament

"I'm a businessman who works from home with early morning calls to make. I get so mad at my son when he dawdles getting out of the house and into the car on the way to school. I've told him a hundred times how important my morning calls are. He's a daydreamer, and my yelling doesn't seem to bother him. An hour should be enough time for anyone to get ready in the morning and out the door."

—Bruce, an impatient and intense father of a slow-adapting and easily distracted ten-year-old

Many different events, thoughts, and emotions can trigger your yelling, but they are all modified or intensified by three unique and important factors: your temperament, your child's temperament, and how they fit together.

In this chapter you'll learn why one of your kids always seems to get under your skin while another one doesn't, or why your neighbor's child is calm and easygoing while your child is raring to go from morning to night. You'll also learn how your own temperament is an important ingredient in what triggers your yelling and in creating power struggles between you and your child.

Looking Through the Lens of Temperament

In the classic book *Your Child Is a Person*, Stella Chess, Alexander Thomas, and Herbert Birch (1977) present the idea that *temperament* is a person's style of behavior. They explain that temperament is not the "what" or the content of behavior, and not the motivation or the "why" of behavior, but "how" we move in the world. It's the way the other aspects of behavior are expressed. Individual temperaments—yours and theirs—influence your day-to-day experiences with your children.

Your child comes into the world with a set of temperament traits that influence the challenges and experiences she faces from infancy on. Over time her temperament may change some based on the environment and the nurturing she receives. Understanding differences in temperament—your own, your partner's, and each child's—can be a revelation, the key that unlocks the door to increasing connection with and compassion toward your child. It can also help you generate strategies to yell less and enjoy your child more.

The Temperament Lens

Thinking about temperament gives you a unique view into behavior. It also provides an understanding about how children learn that may have eluded you.

Imagine it this way: You go to your optometrist, she puts your old prescription lenses in front of your eyes, and you look at a picture of your son. He's blurred and fuzzy, and his behavior is a mystery to you. You realize that your old lenses haven't been letting you see your child clearly. Then she puts the new "temperament lenses" in front of you and asks you to look at your son. Suddenly, your vision clears. You see his smile, the mischievous twinkle in his eye, and the chocolate in the corner of his mouth revealing that he's proud of himself for figuring out how to reach the brownies. You see his strength, his persistence, and his passion to learn. For the first time, you notice how alike you two are. You wonder why it's so easy for you to get mad at him. You ask to keep the temperament lenses in place so you can continue to see and accept your son for who he is.

If you find your child's behavior to be challenging and frustrating most days, learning about temperament will shed light on the difficulties you both face. I wish I'd had this understanding when my own children were young, but it's never too late to learn. I think about temperament often in my interactions with my adult children, my husband, and my grandkids.

Temperament: The Wide Range of Normal

Most experts agree that temperament has a genetic basis: we come into the world with a style all our own. Before the work of psychiatrists Stella Chess and Alexander Thomas (1986)—pioneers in temperament research—parents, especially mothers, were blamed for many behavior problems. Chess and Thomas's highly respected research, the New York Longitudinal Study (1955–85), helped parents and professionals look at children's behavior in a different light. They became convinced that children have innate differences that play a key role in determining each child's behavior. They defined these differences as nine temperament traits: activity level, rhythmicity (or regularity), approach or withdrawal, adaptability, threshold of responsiveness (sensitivity), intensity of reaction, quality of mood, distractibility, and persistence.

Understanding a child's temperament is a way to make sense of behavioral issues, social interactions, preferences, and power struggles. Temperament is not about the motivation for a child's behavior. A child who is highly active most of the time (his temperament) and loves to run is different from a child who runs away from you because he doesn't want to leave the park yet (a motivation for running). How your child approaches a new task or challenge will depend in part on his or her temperament. A cautious child will take longer to warm up to a new babysitter, while an outgoing child who is adaptable will wave goodbye to you as soon as the babysitter gets on the floor to play. Both are normal.

In our culture we often move quickly to pathologize children for behaviors that are within the wide range of normal. A teacher might see a slow-to-warm-up child as sad, but this could just be the child's normal approach to new people and new environments. If the teacher understands that a child who is shy needs to feel comfortable and safe, then an environment and attitude that is welcoming to a cautious child can be offered. Over time the teacher will be able to see if the child's behavior is based on temperament or if an evaluation or intervention is warranted. If a parent and teacher talk early on, they can come up with strategies that will increase a child's comfort level and decrease stress.

Temperament Traits Can Be Seen in Babies

When I worked as a nurse in the postpartum nursery, I observed that some newborns cried softly and rested easily, while others had their fists clenched, squirmed around, and made sure we all came running when they cried loudly. I could see the temperamental differences right away, and I came to know that babies don't come into the world as a "blank slate." Some mothers tell me that they knew they had an active child when their baby was in utero doing gymnastics.

Babies who cry intensely can test your confidence and patience. Just knowing that the cries may be indicative of your child's temperament can help you stay calm and figure out what your baby needs. When I worked as a temperament counselor in the pediatric department at Kaiser Permanente, we offered temperament profiles starting at the age of four months. It helped a great deal to give individualized, anticipatory guidance to parents so they knew what to expect as their child developed.

If you know your child is easily frustrated, you might encourage her to reach for the ball on the floor to stretch her frustration tolerance. If your infant is highly sensitive, chances are you spend many hours trying to soothe him. As he matures, you may choose to teach him how to sleep on his own. This is all to say that learning about temperament when children are young can prepare you for the later years, when you may find yourself yelling more than you thought you would. If your children are already out of diapers, it's never too late to start to understand what makes them tick.

"My Kids Are So Different from Each Other"

Parents are often surprised when their second child is significantly different from their first. You may find that approaches that worked wonders with your first child just don't work with the second. My first son, Pay, would happily eat anything that I put on his plate, but my second child, Mara, had a different point of view. She refused some foods based on the texture and refused to take the occasional bottle offered when I wasn't around to nurse her. I couldn't understand why my children were so different from each other and why the things I tried with one didn't seem to work with the other.

I was a young mother with good instincts, but I had a limited understanding of child development and no knowledge of temperament. Over time I learned to adapt my parenting style based on my children's individual differences. This took trial and error and acceptance of how different my children were. It was a great discovery for me when I finally learned about temperament a few years after my youngest child, Carina, was born. I often wonder why this concept isn't taught in high school to all potential parents.

Although children come into the world with certain temperament traits, sibling relationships have a significant impact on behavior. For example, a child might naturally be low in reactivity and intensity, but because her older sister is highly intense and yells frequently, she quickly learns to match her and yell to be heard. Another child might withdraw from his sibling's intensity instead of imitating it.

It takes observation and curiosity to understand the role temperament plays in your child's life. It's hard to know if a particular behavior (such as having a tantrum at the store) is because of your child's temperament (intensity), an environmental factor (loud noise and crowds), an internal need (hunger), a developmental stage (a two-year-old who wants everything), or past experience (discomfort in the shopping cart). Behavior is like a puzzle with many pieces, and when you put them together, you get a rich and complex picture of your child. Temperament is a vital piece of the puzzle, and over time your child's behavior will be a little bit more predictable.

Identifying and Accepting Individual Differences

A key to any healthy relationship is accepting other people for who they are! When we try to make someone fit into our idea of what a perfect child, husband, wife, mother, sibling, or friend should be, we are bound to be disappointed when he or she doesn't live up to our expectations. When you observe and learn about your child's unique style, you can then adapt your reactions, discipline, and expectations according to your child's needs.

It's equally important to understand your own temperament and how it fits with your child's temperaments. Seeing your similarities and differences will provide you with insights that will lead to fewer power struggles and less yelling.

Understanding Your Child's Temperament

Exercise 4.1 is a quick survey of temperament. Think about your child's usual reactions on an average day. If you have a spouse or parenting partner, have him or her do this survey separately. Don't discuss it until after you are done. Afterward, compare notes and see if you perceive your child in the same way.

This can be a fruitful and perhaps surprising conversation to have. Parents often perceive their children differently, based on their own temperament and experiences. For example, if you're the organized, sensitive, and persistent parent who does more of the daily care and discipline, and your partner is the active, flexible, easygoing weekend parent, your perceptions of your children are bound to be different.

Exercise 4.1 outlines nine temperament traits. *Remember, there are no good or bad traits—everyone has some aspect of each trait as a part of their temperament style.* Circle the number that best fits your child. Don't worry if you're not sure; just make a good guess. Doing this survey is a way to polish your temperament lenses and look at your child with fresh eyes. (A downloadable copy of the survey is available at http://www .newharbinger.com/29071. See the back of the book for more details on how to access it.)

EXERCISE 4.1: General Impressions of Your Child's Temperament

1. Sensitivity

How sensitive is your child to noise, temperature, light, the taste of food, or the texture of things? Is your child particular about how clothing feels? Is she easily overwhelmed? Does she notice small differences in her environment? Or do most things just roll off her back? *(A child could be a 5 if highly sensitive to noise or touch for example, but not to other things.)*

1	2	3	4	5
low sensitivity				high sensitivity

2. Activity

Does your child have lots of energy and always seem to be on the go? Does your child have trouble playing quietly and prefer to be active? Or is your child quiet and able to spend extended time in activities that don't require much moving and talking? *(High-activity children can also sit quietly for videos or engaging activities.)*

1	2	3	4	5
low activity				high activity

3. Intensity

Does your child have strong emotional reactions? Is your child expressive with feelings or more reserved, mellow, and hard to read? *(Intense children feel the highs and the lows of life with passion.)*

1	2	3	4	5
low intensity				high intensity

4. Adaptability

Is your child able to adapt quickly to changes, transitions, or expectations? Or is it difficult for your child when there is a new routine or schedule? Does your child have trouble when it's time to start or stop an activity, or is he flexible and able to go with the flow most of the time? *(Slow-adapting children are natural planners; they have a picture of how things should go that may not match your picture.)*

1	2	3	4	5
fast adapting				slow adapting

5. Mood

Is your child happy and in a good mood most of the time, or is she more serious, focusing on the negative more often? *(Mood is sometimes also based on the other traits and on how well a child fits with the environment.)*

1	2	3	4	5
happy				serious

6. Approach/Withdrawal

What is your child's first and usual reaction to new people, situations, ideas, or places? Does she jump right in, or is she cautious? *(When cautious children feel comfortable, they warm up even to strange places and people.)*

1	2	3	4	5
outgoing (extrovert)			cautious/slow to warm up (introvert)	

7. Persistence

Does your child stick with things even when tired or you've told him to stop? Or does he get frustrated and give up easily? How long will he continue to make an effort? *(You might have a child who is persistent when he wants something but gets frustrated easily for other things.)*

1	2	3	4	5
persistent (manages frustration)				not persistent (gets easily frustrated)

8. Regularity or Rhythmicity

Does your child normally eat, sleep, wake up, and eliminate at the same time each day? Is your child predictable? Or is your child flexible and unpredictable? *(Watch and see what your child is like on the weekend when you don't impose the schedule like you do on school days.)*

1	2	3	4	5
regular				irregular

9. Distractibility

Is your child easily distracted by noises and people? Does your child forget to do what you said when something else catches his attention? Can you distract your child from upset feelings or from things that are off limits? Or does your child focus on a task without being easily distracted? *(Children who are easily distracted are often highly perceptive.)*

1	2	3	4	5
easily distracted				not easily distracted

Note: Adapted with permission by James Cameron, PhD, and David Rice, PhD, of the Preventive Ounce, 1994. The model of temperament used here was derived from the work of Stella Chess, MD, and Alexander Thomas, MD, in the New York Longitudinal Study. The concept of General Impressions was derived from temperament questionnaires developed by William B. Carey, MD, and Sean C. McDevitt, PhD, and associates. This scale is not intended to replace a complete temperament assessment, which can be obtained from various sources. You can find more information in the resource section of this book.

Understanding Your Own Temperament

Once you have circled all nine traits for your child, go back to the beginning of the survey and do it for your own temperament. Put a different symbol (a square or triangle) around the numbers that represent *your* temperament.

Focus on your natural style, not what you have to do at work or at school. Over the years, you've learned to adapt to the expectations of your environment and family members, but try to think about your authentic style. Perhaps you're an active person but have found yourself in a job where you have to sit at a computer most of the day. You've adapted out of necessity, but on the weekends you want to go, go, go. You might rate yourself as a four or five on the activity scale.

Take some time to reflect on the temperament traits that you have marked for you and your child. Think about any conflicts you are having and the ways in which you get along great. About any situation you want to explore, ask yourself, *What's temperament got to do with it?* There's a good chance you've never looked at how you relate to your child in quite this way. You can also go back and use a different symbol to mark another family member. You will develop a useful map of some of your family dynamics.

For example, when I first learned about temperament and did the survey, I understood more clearly why my daughter Mara had a hard time with how loud my husband and I talked and argued. She is more sensitive than either of us, and our yelling really bothered her. I think it scared all of our kids, but the more sensitive a child is, the more it can affect her. My husband, who's an actor, didn't think that his firm voice was yelling, even when everyone in the family experienced it as such. He was known to say on occasion, "I'm not yelling! Do you want to hear what yelling sounds like?"

By looking through the temperament lens, I also understood why my intense, fast-paced speech and movement was challenging for my youngest daughter. Carina is slower-paced and more mild mannered than I am. She reminds me to slow down, listen, and give her a chance to finish what she wants to say before I start to talk. I find that helpful and still challenging to do.

Perhaps you're sensitive, and when you hear your wife and son argue, you feel like running out of the house. They may not think their yelling is a big deal, but it really bugs you. Maybe your daughter is the dramatic type, and when she tries to get you engaged with her intensity, you just withdraw or yell in response to her demands.

Spend time reflecting on how your temperament works with the other members of the family. You may have an aha moment, a new way of understanding your relationship with your child. When I teach a temperament workshop, someone always says something like, "Wow. I never realized my child was so similar to me. No wonder we butt heads—we're both so strong willed." Or, "Looks like my son is cut from the same cloth as my husband. When I got married, I didn't know I would be living with two intense and sensitive men someday."

The Fit Between Your Child's Temperament and Your Temperament

Now that you have an idea of your child's temperament and how it fits with yours, you can decide what to focus on as you look at each situation through the lens of temperament. There are ways to "stretch" your child's natural style of doing things, but the first step is to give up unrealistic expectations.

Goodness of Fit

The way in which your child's temperament meshes with yours might produce a good fit or a poor fit. When there is a poor fit, conflict and power struggles are more likely. And as the parent, it's up to you to work toward a better fit.

"Healthy functioning and development occurs when there is a goodness of fit between the capacities and characteristics of the individual and the demands and expectations of the environment" (Chess and Thomas 1986, 12). When you change the environment and the demands put on your child in a way that fits better with his or her temperament, there will be less misbehavior and as a result you'll be triggered less. Understanding the relationship between temperament and behavior should help to reduce any guilt and blame either you or your child experiences. You will still find challenges to manage, such as a slow-adapting child who needs to leave the house on time or a sensitive child at a loud party. If you know your child is easily frustrated, you can help her get started on her homework, have her work on things she can do, and stay nearby to help when needed. If you get frustrated easily as well, you might consider hiring a homework helper or asking a relative to do homework with her a few times a week.

If you understand your child's temperament, you can take a proactive approach and work to prepare your child for an upcoming situation. Over time and with practice, you and your child will learn how to adapt to challenging situations.

What's Happening at School?

When you look at goodness of fit, also think about a child's school environment. A highly active child who is required to sit for long periods of time may be seen as having a behavior problem when he fidgets and squirms. Once he is moved to a different classroom, where sitting for long periods of time is not expected, his problems may disappear because the expectations and the environment fit well for him. One teacher may be more flexible in style than another.

If a child who is sensitive is placed in a large and loud preschool setting, his resistance to going to school may increase because of the overstimulation in the environment. Perhaps you will come to see that yelling at him in the morning to get ready doesn't address his underlying discomfort in his school environment. When you take a step back from yelling, you have the opportunity to get a new perspective on your child's behavior and the changes in the environment that are needed.

Rona's Wakeup Call

I learned to reduce my intensity with my children in part because I saw how my anger and yelling hurt them. I felt like I had to do the changing before I could teach them to do something differently.

One day, when my son Matt was around four, he was in a particularly active and unfocused mood. He was not really sure what he wanted to do while I talked with my friend, who had stopped by to chat. He kept coming over to me to ask a question or demand something. I tried to redirect him, but he was unhappy with not having a friend to play with. He provoked me until I yelled at him and then, without thinking, I hit him. I had yelled at him before, but I had never hit him. I saw his tears and the shocked look on his face. My friend was also quite surprised and quickly said she had to take off. I was embarrassed, ashamed, and devastated about losing control and hurting my son.

This experience was a wakeup call for me. My intensity was often an asset in my life, but it was a trait I needed to learn to manage as a parent. I had unfortunately yelled at and spanked my older son when I was stressed as a single mom, but thought I was past that.

I didn't realize how Matt's intensity was triggering my own, and how important it was to help him get settled before I became engrossed in a conversation with my friend. That day I promised myself to never spank again, and I didn't. It took longer for me to learn how to lower my intensity enough to not yell. Over time, I came to understand the power of saying, "I'm starting to feel really angry right now, so I need a few minutes to cool off. I'll be right back."

How Temperament Influences Yelling

Here are some ways that temperament can impact your yelling. Make note of examples that resonate with you. Use the temperament survey to think about the relationships between your temperament, your child's temperament, your propensity to yell, and the effect on your child.

- If one child is sensitive, your yelling may worry him more than it does your other child.

- If your daughter is intense, you may find she triggers your yelling daily, especially if you're intense as well. When you yell, her reactivity increases.

- If you are low in activity and sensitive and if your kids love to run around the house, yelling may come easily when you just want some peace and quiet.

- If you are fast adapting and your son is slow adapting to transitions and changes, your impatience may set off yelling on a daily basis.

- If you are the life of the party, your daughter's shyness may irritate you enough that you yell and say things to her that you later regret.

- If your son is moody and doesn't smile when his grandparents come to visit, your disappointment may lead to yelling once they leave.

- If you are easily frustrated and your daughter is strong willed, power struggles may occur when she wants something and won't let up.

- If you are a flexible person, your son's insistence on knowing what's going to happen and when it's going to happen may be foreign to you, especially when he has to eat, poop, and go to sleep the same time every day. When you yell, he gets more rigid.

After you spend time thinking about temperament, you're likely to deepen your compassion for your child's experience. You may have a greater appreciation for how hard your child works to learn how to function in a world that is often confusing, demanding, and at times frightening.

It's essential to develop compassion for yourself as well, as you witness your mistakes, distractions, frustrations, and inexperience. You will yell less if you keep the individual differences of your family members in your mind and heart.

Different Styles: Maya and Her Daughter, Anna

Maya, a working mother of two, is innately sensitive and slow to warm up. Her natural style is to refuel by being alone, and she prefers quiet evenings at home. Her job as a kindergarten teacher has made her more outgoing in her classroom. Her coworkers would be surprised to hear that she thinks of herself as shy, cautious, and sensitive. She is neat and orderly and finds comfort in sticking to a daily routine, even though that's been difficult since she became a parent.

Her daughter, Anna, is a loud and dramatic six-year-old who always wants to engage with her mama. She is impulsive and easily distracted, so she doesn't stay with one activity for very long. Anna usually starts to bug Maya to play a game with her as soon as they walk in the house after school. Maya falls into the trap of begging her to find something to play with and then the begging quickly leads to yelling when Anna won't let up (she's high in persistence). Another pattern of Anna's is to pick on her younger brother when she's frustrated, in part because she wants a little excitement and interaction. Anna's loud voice and her brother's fussing really grate on Maya's nerves, causing her to retreat or yell. Maya rarely has time to run or exercise anymore, and she feels like she's getting grouchier by the day.

What follows is the temperament survey Maya filled out for herself and her daughter, Anna. You can see that Maya and Anna are very different in many ways.

Maya's traits are noted by the triangle (▼) and her daughter Anna's, by the circle (●).

1. Sensitivity

●Daughter   Mother▼

1	2	3	4	5
low sensilivity				high sensitivity

2. Activity

          Mother ▼   ● Daughter

1	2	3	4	5
low activity				high activity

3. Intensity

          Mother ▼   ● Daughter

1	2	3	4	5
low intensity				high intensity

4. Adaptability

                    ● Daughter   Mother▼

1	2	3	4	5
fast adapting				slow adapting

5. Mood

          Mother ▼   ● Daughter

1	2	3	4	5
happy				serious

6. Approach/Withdrawal

● Daughter   Mother ▼

1	2	3	4	5
outgoing			cautious/slow to warm up	
(extrovert)			(introvert)	

7. Persistence

● Daughter   Mother ▼

1	2	3	4	5
persistent			not persistent	
(manages frustration)			(gets easily frustrated)	

8. Regularity or Rhythmicity

Mother ▼   ● Daughter

1	2	3	4	5
regular				irregular

9. Distractibility

● Daughter   Mother ▼

1	2	3	4	5
easily distracted			not easily distracted	

Maya can't change who her daughter is, but she can learn new problem-solving and coping strategies to support her desire to yell less. Here are a few examples.

Maya prepares herself for the transition from work to being with her kids. She asks the babysitter to stay longer with her son, and she picks up Anna from school and spends an hour with her before they go home. Some days they go to the nearby lake for a little jog and an afternoon snack, or they enjoy going to the farmers market or to the library.

This one-on-one time with Mom really calms Anna down. When they get home, Anna has a schedule that she helped work on, so she knows how the late afternoon and evening will go. Mom signs Anna up for a soccer camp on Saturdays, and during that time Maya sits in the grass watching the game and plays with her toddler. Afterward, Anna is often invited to go to a friend's house for a playdate, giving Maya more time to refuel while her son naps.

Maya has also started to use a timer to help Anna wait when Mom says, "I'll be able to play with you in ten minutes." Anna has a new voice recorder that she sings into, and she can send recordings to her grandparents for entertainment. This keeps her happy when Mom is busy, and she even goes to her room to rehearse and get into costume. She loves doing a show for the family after dinner.

The power struggles they were having are less frequent now that Maya feels much more relaxed and accepting of Anna. Maya has also learned that if she doesn't take care of some of her own needs, resentment builds, and then she struggles to enjoy her kids. She knows that Anna's intensity can be channeled into creative experiences, providing more pleasure for everyone. There is less yelling when Maya can think ahead and set up an environment that offers comfort and stimulation.

Power Struggles Fueled by Temperament

Do you ever feel like you are holding on to one end of a rope, your child is on the other end, and both of you are pulling as hard as you can to win? Tug-of-war is not much fun with children who insist on having their way every time you say, "It's time to do homework. Clean up this mess! It's bedtime! Good morning, time to wake up. Get in the car!"

Power struggles are common in families, and they often lead to yelling, nagging, threats, or punishment. Ongoing conflict with your child will leave you feeling exhausted. If you are always the strongest and most powerful in the tug-of-war, your child will become more distant, feel defeated and powerless, and may even become more defiant. If your child tends to win the power struggles, he will learn to pull harder, louder, and more often, and your anger will increase.

In a power struggle, each person holds on to his or her position, demand, or belief and is unwilling to listen to the other person or come up with a solution. During a power struggle you might think, *If I don't stand up for what's right, I'll be seen as weak. If I give in, I'll get walked all over. I'm not that kind of parent.* Often the original subject of the struggle is lost and the focus becomes *Who will win?*

Your temperament and your child's may be key ingredients that fuel your power struggles. Here is an example of Manny and his daughter Marika. Both of them are strong willed.

• Manny and Marika's Story

One afternoon, Manny calls from the kitchen, where he has just started getting dinner prepared, "Marika, it's almost five and time to start your homework."

Marika's response is a familiar one: "In a minute, I just have to finish my drawing."

After a few minutes, Manny sees that Marika is still drawing and hasn't started her homework. He thinks about how it's going to be another rushed evening trying to get homework done before they go to her piano lesson. He has escalating thoughts about Marika always trying to get her way and being spoiled. He yells loudly, "Marika, I told you to stop what you're doing and start your homework NOW! Do what I say, or you'll be sorry."

Marika replies, "All right," but she ignores her father's request and keeps drawing. She knows that he will continue to work on dinner and watch the news before he comes back into the room and insist she stop. She really wants to finish the picture she is working on so she can show it to her friends at school.

Ten minutes later Manny comes back into the living room and yells, "I'm sick and tired of you not listening to me. You must stop right now or else there's no lesson. What's wrong with you?" Marika looks up at her father and with determination and frustration in her voice says, "I don't care about my stupid lesson. Don't you understand that I have to finish my drawing? I don't see why you have to be in charge of everything I do."

Manny is pretty worked up by now and yells, "That's enough, young lady. You can't do whatever you want in this house. Now get up to your room this minute and start your homework. There won't be any more drawing."

He grabs her pencils and paper and continues to yell, "Drawing pictures won't get you a scholarship for college."

Under her breath Marika mumbles, "I hate you. You're the meanest father in the whole world." Marika has art supplies in her room, so she plans on getting her drawing and working on it tonight when she's supposed to be asleep.

Manny's relevant temperament traits are his distractibility, high intensity, and fast adaptability. Marika is persistent, low in distractibility and sensitivity. She doesn't like it when her father yells, but she's usually able to tune him out and ignore his requests. She is quite focused when it comes to her art. When Marika ignores her father, his intensity rises, he gets impatient, and his need to win the battle increases. They are both committed to their goals, but it's really important to Marika to finish what she has started.

Deconstructing Power Struggles

I'm sure you can already see ways for Manny to approach his daughter that wouldn't lead to a power struggle. He could

- talk to Marika face-to-face about the schedule, instead of calling from the other room;

- ask her for her input about how to get everything done;

- listen to his daughter's needs;

- respond in a positive way to the artwork she was so focused on, and then come up with a plan for when she could finish her drawing after getting her homework done;

- reduce his intensity by taking a minute to pause and get clear on his priorities and goals.

Of course, it's so much easier to see what to do when you're not the one being defied or ignored. In the moment, you may lose track of what's most important. Although Marika's persistence, low distractibility, and creativity add to the power struggle with her dad, these traits are also strengths that can lead to great accomplishments in her life. If Manny had a better sense of his own traits, he might know how to harness his daughter's strong will and get things done without losing his temper. Understanding temperament is essential in reducing power struggles.

Temperament is not the only lens to look through when you want to deconstruct a power struggle. Look at the stress levels you and your child are under. Ask yourself if either of you is hungry. Did you get enough sleep last night? Have you connected and had time for affection or fun? What else is going on for your child and for you that might propel you toward a tug-of-war? Have you taken the time to listen to your child, to acknowledge what she's feeling, and to express your needs as well?

We will discuss other ways to avoid power struggles in chapter 7. An excellent resource for an in-depth look at power struggles is *Kids, Parents, and Power Struggles: Winning for a Lifetime* (Kurcinka 2000).

A Thought to Consider:
I set the tone.

As the parent, you set the tone. Your response to your child leads the way and gives a clue to your child about how to respond. Check in with yourself to make sure you are setting the tone you really want. If your child is spinning out of control, your ability to stay calm will matter.

As you become familiar with your temperament and your child's temperament, you will start to recognize the ways you both get challenged and triggered. You will also recognize your strengths and your child's strengths. Stretch your temperament, become more flexible, and reach out to your child. Instead of giving in to impatience, allow your child a few minutes to finish a game. Like a tree, you can bend with the wind and weather the storms that come your way. (Please see the appendix for a tree meditation that can help you with this.)

Part 2

Everyday Strategies for Yelling Less

"The most precious gift we can offer anyone is our attention. When mindfulness embraces those we love, they will bloom like flowers."

—Thich Nhat Hanh

Now that you've worked through the chapters in part 1, you understand more about why you yell and the impact it has on your family. Now you are ready to take significant steps to change some of your patterns and reactions.

In this section we'll talk about how you can track your yelling, observe your own patterns, and use that information to develop strategies for yelling less that you can put into practice right away. These approaches will also help you implement long-term behavioral change, and your ability to stay calm will grow.

As you read the following chapters, keep your child's unique temperament in mind, and refer back to chapter 4 as needed. This will deepen your understanding of how temperament impacts behavior—both yours and your child's. Temperament specialist Mary Sheedy Kurcinka (2001, 169) reminds us, "Working with your child's type is often like a dance—two steps forward, one back, pause, step again. The more familiar the steps, the easier to dance."

Over time you will develop new ways to communicate, connect, and get things done.

Chapter 5

"Yelling Is So Easy ... Can I Really Stop?"

Observing and Gathering Data for Success

"Every time my son doesn't do the dishes when he's supposed to, I get angry and yell. I can feel the tension start in my neck and move right into my throat. It's like a flame ignites, and I become a fire-breathing dragon ready to attack. Sometimes I can walk away when I notice my tension rising. Most of the time, I yell."

—Tess, mother of a twelve-year-old boy

When you begin to notice *in the moment* what you do and how you feel when you yell at your child, and you don't judge yourself harshly for it, you've taken a big leap in the right direction. Discovering the patterns of your feelings, thoughts, and reactions will give you basic information you can use to develop strategies for change.

These patterns and bits of information are invaluable. Think of yourself as a scientist: let curiosity and necessity lead the way to new discoveries and new ways of doing things.

Tracking Your Yelling

Tracking—paying attention to your triggers and your responses over time, and writing down what happens—is an effective tool for changing your behavior. Professionals in a variety of fields use tracking to help their clients reach their goals. Nutritionists use tracking to help people lose weight, financial consultants have clients track spending, and sleep consultants use tracking to help parents develop new bedtime routines and habits so children learn to sleep soundly. Bringing awareness to what you actually do is the foundation for changing habits.

The following is an example of a situation that happened frequently to Gabby, a mother of two, and of how tracking helped her learn to communicate respectfully.

• Gabby's Story

Gabby has two sons, ages four and seven. Most mornings she winds up yelling at them to get their shoes on before school. The boys dawdle, ignore her, and keep playing. She rushes them out of the house at the last minute, yelling at them for not being ready, while helping them get their shoes on. It's a stressful way to start the day, and although she doesn't like it, she figures it's what she has to do to get them to school on time.

As Gabby begins to track her yelling, she sees that morning is the hardest time for her. She gets the kids ready by herself and knows that she should prepare more the night before. She has many things to do in the evening once the kids are asleep, and most nights she flops on her bed after 11 p.m., energy spent.

Gabby's key temperament traits are high distractibility, high energy, irregularity, and high intensity. Her boys are moderate in energy, intensity, and sensitivity. The younger one is fast adapting and the older one, slow adapting. Most mornings the boys get involved in playing with their train set after breakfast. The older one has a hard time stopping when Mom says it's time for school, and the younger one does whatever his big brother is doing.

Getting their shoes on is a signal that it's time for them to stop playing and leave for school, so it's natural that they would resist if they're having fun. They easily tune out Mom's yelling, since they are not sensitive, and her intensity doesn't seem to bother them right away.

Gabby begins to see that she is stuck in a rut. As she tracks her yelling, she identifies the pattern that she has developed since she went back to work a few months ago. Before that, she didn't rush around the house trying to do two things at once, and she was much less stressed. She now sees that yelling from another room is the first sign that the storm is just around the corner. After a little practice, Gabby is able to catch her escalating thoughts when the kids don't respond to her first round of, "Get your shoes on!"

Gabby's thoughts were familiar ones: *They're spoiled brats who think they can just tune me out. I loved going to school when I was their age ... What's wrong with them? Why can't they just listen so I can get going?* Catching them, Gabby is surprised by her own negativity.

Whenever she rushed around thinking she would be late, all reason seemed to leave her. She also noticed that she got more distracted and couldn't find her keys or phone when she was in that state of mind. She would feel lightheaded and tense; both clues, she realized, meant that she needed to have something to eat before leaving the house.

One day she took a few deep breaths, sat down on her bed, and started talking to herself. She found herself saying, "They're just kids. They play so well together. I'm a lucky mom." She took a few more full breaths and decided that she would stop yelling and go into their room to see what she could do instead. When she walked in, the boys were happily playing. She sat on the floor and just watched them for about thirty seconds, continuing her easy breaths. That's all the time that was needed. They looked at her, the little one jumped in her lap, and her older son showed her his new train track design. Then, she calmly said it was time to get shoes on and that after school she would like to hear more about their train adventure. She helped the little one, as her older son put his shoes on. It didn't take any more time than yelling at them would have taken to sit and connect before getting them out of the house. And she walked out the door feeling like it was going to be a good day.

Tracking Works

In the next chapter we'll discuss in more detail the process of noticing your feelings and thoughts and doing something to change how you respond to your kids. Right now, you have the opportunity to begin tracking your own triggers and reactions, as Gabby did.

Tracking is a great way to increase your awareness and acceptance of the habits and reactions that you want to change. If you can be honest with yourself while also being compassionate, there is no doubt in my mind that you will yell less.

EXERCISE: Track Your Yelling

Use the Yelling Tracker form (Figure 5.1) to track your yelling. Make copies of the Yelling Tracker from this book, or go to http://www.newharbinger .com/29071 to download a copy for your computer or mobile device. (See the back of the book for more details about download.) You can also adapt the tracker to the format best suited for you. For example, you might prefer to use a spreadsheet or to keep your information in a diary.

Use the tracker for at least a week. Tracking for even more time would be helpful to gather information. If you feel resistant to tracking, consider committing to doing it for one day, and then commit to another day. If the process seems overwhelming, you can also focus on one of the tracking steps at a time and add another as you get used to it.

1. Set a start date for tracking. Be prepared with copies of the form or whatever you decide to use.

2. Fill out the tracker on the same day that the yelling occurs so you can remember exactly what went on. You may be able to do this right away, you may need to wait until the kids are in bed, or you may be able to take a few minutes while they're doing their homework or playing. If another parent lives at home who also yells, see if he or she will agree to track as well.

Event

> Trigger Event
>
> Day
>
> Time
>
> Place

Your Reactions

> Your physical reaction
>
> Your emotions
>
> Your escalating thoughts

Responses

> Your response to the trigger event (what did you do?)
>
> Your child's response to your yelling

Temperament Traits at Play

> Yours
>
> Your child's

Aftermath

> After you yelled, how did you feel?
>
> How did your child feel?

Evaluation

> What could you have done differently?

Figure 5.1. Yelling Tracker

Some of the ideas for this tracker came from the book *When Anger Hurts Your Kids* (McKay et al. 1996).

How James Used the Yelling Tracker

In chapter 4 you read about James, who yelled at his two-year-old daughter, Sasha, when she was eating. Although James realized that some of the causes of his yelling were coming from his childhood experiences, he needed more tools to respond differently to his daughter. The examples below show how James filled out his yelling tracker.

Step 1: Note the Event

Start with simple facts. These clues hold valuable information. They are like puzzle pieces. When you put them together, you begin to see the full picture.

Event

> **Trigger Event** *Sasha throws her food on the floor, looks at me, and laughs.*
>
> **Day** *Monday*   **Time** *8 AM*
>
> **Place** *Kitchen*

Trigger Event: Make a brief note about what behavior set you off. This is key to seeing the patterns that have developed for you and other family members.

Day: Over time, you may discover that you have more challenges on certain days. If you see a pattern developing, try to figure out what is different about that day of the week or the night before. For example, you might work late on Tuesday nights and sleep in Wednesday mornings, causing you to rush, nag, and yell more than usual. Or perhaps you find you're more irritable on Monday, when your workload is heavy and your kids have too much homework.

Time: Do you have a witching hour? Does your child act out more at a certain time of day? Perhaps you yell more on the mornings when you haven't had time to make your coffee and your partner goes to work early. Or perhaps you only yell when you're trying to get the kids to bed. If you have to referee another evening battle or beg to get teeth brushed, you explode.

Place: Where does your yelling occur? Is the car the place you let loose, or is it only in the kitchen during meals? You might see that when you're outside, you don't yell much, but when you walk through the front door and see that your house is a mess, you lose your playful self.

Step 2: Note Your Reactions

The next step is to notice your physical reactions, your emotions, and your escalating thoughts. What occurs as you respond to a trigger is not linear. You may not experience things in this order. For example, you may sense changes in your body after you become aware of your thoughts or before you notice how you're feeling.

Your Reactions

Your physical reaction

I clenched my jaw & folded my arms.

Your emotions *I felt angry and impatient.*

Your escalating thoughts

"I'll never get to work on time"
"She is making a mess."

Your Physical Reactions: Being able to tune into your body's reactions can help you put your yelling brakes on. Scan your body after a trigger event and see where you are holding tension. As your anger rises, your body will respond. Notice your posture, gestures, tone of voice, and breathing.

James has a good clue he can use to yell less. If he notices his arms folding, then that can cue him to check in on his feelings and thoughts. You might also practice noticing what your body feels and looks like in ordinary conversations when you're not yelling and you're feeling relaxed. This is part of becoming familiar with yourself.

Your Emotions: You may not have learned to identify your emotions growing up, so it may take some practice to become aware of how you're feeling. Anger is the most common emotion people feel before they yell, but other emotions may be simmering just under the surface. If you can say to yourself, "I'm getting angry or impatient," then you might have the presence of mind to step away and cool off.

94

Your Escalating Thoughts: It takes practice to become aware of what you're telling yourself that fuels the fire. As James worries about work and the mess Sasha has made, he becomes angrier, and the tension in his body builds. His thoughts have a great impact on his actions.

Step 3: Note Your Responses

Here is the part where you work to observe without judgment. You're not on trial. You are doing your best to be honest about the way you respond to your child's behavior, needs, or demands.

Responses

> **Your response to the trigger event (what did you do?)** *after the 2nd time she threw food I yelled, "No more playing around! You are not getting any more food! I have had enough." I was very loud.*
>
> **Your child's response to your yelling**
>
> *She looked at me and she started to cry, and she arched her back.*

Your Response: Tracking what you do will help you see your patterns and learn what doesn't work. If you used hurtful words, write them down. Reflect on why you think you chose these words. Remind yourself that you are working to break these patterns and that there are many times during the week when you are kind and loving toward your child.

Your Child's Response: As noted in previous chapters, your child's response may help you stay motivated to yell less. Some children will be reactive; others will withdraw.

Step 4: Note the Aftermath

Parents often report feeling bad after they yell. How is it for you? Write down whatever you feel, and try not to censor yourself.

Aftermath

> **After you yelled, how did you feel?**
>
> *Ashamed, angry with myself for losing it.*
>
> **How did your child feel?**
>
> *She was upset by my yelling. She calmed down when I picked her up, hugged her, & apologized.*

Your Feelings: After you yell, how do you feel? Your feelings can change quickly. You may move from feeling angry to feeling ashamed, sad, relieved, or frustrated. Become familiar with your feelings so you can feel them without fear.

Your Child's Feelings: How does your child feel? Paying attention to your emotions and your child's will guide you in your actions. A child who is angry after you've yelled may need to hear you say that you are sorry about yelling and that you understand his feelings. He may need some time to cool off before you talk about it any further. A child who looks sad may need a hug and some words of reassurance that you love her. Later on, when you're both calm, you can work with her to stop the undesirable behavior. In the next chapter we'll explore alternatives to yelling.

Step 5: Note Temperament Traits at Play

You and your child may be "too much alike" for comfort, or so different that you don't understand each other.

Temperament Traits at Play

Yours

Sensitive
intense
fast-adapting
regular

Your child's

Persistent
intense
irregular
slow-adapting

Your Temperament: James realizes that his high sensitivity and desire to have things regular and orderly contribute to his strong reaction to Sasha throwing her food on the floor. Also, his intensity goes up when he can't get things done at the pace he would like. He's fast adapting, and she is slow adapting, a frequent setup for frustration and yelling.

Your Child's Temperament: Because Sasha is persistent and slow to adapt, she usually won't stop the first time James asks her to. She is passionate about trying new things and having fun. Like her dad, she has strong reactions when she's upset.

Step 6: Note Your Evaluation

In the next chapter we will focus on the vital question *What could I have done differently*? If a new solution occurs to you now, jot it down; but remember that your main task at this point is simply to gather the data.

Evaluation

What could you have done differently?

I could have walked away and calmed down.

If at any time you feel overwhelmed by tracking, just pick one step to focus on, and then gradually add the others as you feel more comfortable. Take your time. You are breaking patterns that took a long time to develop. With two steps forward, one step back, and two more forward, you will make progress.

Track the Storm and Know When It's Building

Anger will often catch you by surprise. Before you know it, you feel "taken over" by it. As you track your yelling, you are looking for that moment when frustration caused by your child's behavior turns into a feeling that is intense and seems to have a life of its own.

If you can sense your emotions getting strong, and you are able to pay attention to your bodily reactions and thoughts, it is possible to calm the storm before it becomes a hurricane and does some damage to the relationship you have with your kids.

Emotions are normal—we all have them. The hard work you are doing is to notice them, accept them, sense them, and learn to not let them dictate your actions. This is essential to yelling less. And remember that any damage done to your relationship can usually be repaired over time. Be kind to yourself as you observe. You are human.

Self-Compassion

In the book *The Mindful Path to Self-Compassion*, clinical psychologist Christopher K. Germer (2009, 28) says, "When we're suffering and feel the urge to help ourselves, we're experiencing self-compassion." Self-compassion—understanding and forgiving yourself—is essential to developing or deepening acceptance for what you observe about your yelling.

If you feel compassion toward yourself and are willing to accept your imperfections, you are less likely to make excuses about your yelling. You may be tempted to make excuses in order to push away feelings of guilt or shame when you see things as they are. For example, you yell at your child for spilling her juice and then hear yourself say something like, "I'm usually not this angry, but I can't help it—we're both sick today." You're tired, you couldn't get anyone to help you, you resent having a sick child, and you're afraid you'll get behind in work. Feeling sick can easily make you more irritable, but it's not an excuse for yelling at your child.

Understanding what you need and your feelings can bring you relief and comfort. You can become compassionate toward yourself and your child. Don't punish yourself for your imperfections. See if you can notice, accept, and then quiet your internal judge after you have yelled or made a mistake. It sounds simple, but most people have never been taught how to do this. If you can learn to be kind to yourself you will also be able to model this skill and attitude for your child.

How Would You Treat Your Friend?

We often have more perspective in dealing with our friends or acquaintances than we do when dealing with our own family members or ourselves. Think about what you might do in the following instance.

Your neighbor, Rosalie, comes to your house upset after an argument with her teenage daughter, who was begging for a sleepover on a school night. "I yelled; I really lost it," Rosalie says miserably. When her daughter yelled back, Rosalie grounded her.

You can see by the way Rosalie looks and sounds that she feels terrible for not being able to communicate with her daughter without yelling. She admits that her daughter was just being a strong-willed teen, wanting to be with her friend, not really doing anything worth a meltdown. Rosalie is usually an accommodating mother, but sometimes when she gets pushed into a corner by her children's persistence, she explodes.

Would you comfort Rosalie? Or would you point out all of her mistakes and make her feel worse?

Chances are you would remind her that she's a good mom and that things happen. You can see that she feels remorse for being harsh toward her daughter. Maybe you tell her that you've walked in her shoes, so you sense how she might feel. You offer her a cup of tea, something to eat, and a hug. You can see that she feels better with your kind words and attention. She sees that she's not alone and that you still like her, even though she's feeling down on herself.

Chances are you know how to be compassionate toward a friend. Now it's time to practice using that kind of attitude and care toward yourself. You are reading this book because you have a desire to treat your child with love and respect, and to do that, you need to give yourself love and respect as well.

Developing Self-Compassion

In her book *Self-Compassion*, Kristin Neff, a researcher and professor at the University of Texas at Austin, explores the many aspects of self-compassion. She helps us understand the importance of self-kindness—being gentle toward ourselves, not judgmental. She suggests that we also realize that we have suffering in common with others. I've noticed that when I realize my connection to humanity and that I'm not alone, my self-judgment dissipates. Another important part is becoming aware of yourself, including your pain. You don't exaggerate or dismiss your suffering. You continue to accept what is true without getting swept away by emotions (Neff 2011).

I bring up the concept of self-compassion now because you will be tracking things that you may not want to see or feel. On this journey, be sure to bring self-compassion along.

Take a moment to answer this question: How can I be compassionate toward myself?

As I'm writing and thinking about this for myself, it occurs to me to look at a certain children's book on my bookshelf in which every page shows a different baby with different emotions. I look at the babies, and I remember that I too was once a beautiful, innocent child. I then imagine holding myself as an infant and gently rocking her. I let myself stay with this image for a minute or two, feeling grateful for who I was and for who I have become. I am sensing myself in a gentle and soft way, instead of being tense. I have a moment of self-compassion that eases the stress I feel in my body and mind. You can go to http://www.newharbinger.com/29071 to download guided meditations for self-compassion and grounding, and you can read the transcripts for those meditations in the appendix. After you listen to the meditations or read them, you can use them any time you need to feel more compassionate, grounded, or flexible.

This way of feeling compassionate may not be right for you. It may feel silly or awkward. But if you sit for a minute and think, "How can I be compassionate toward myself?" you will discover ways to develop self-compassion that fit with your personality. See if you can keep this question in mind for a few minutes each day. Put a reminder on your computer, phone, or refrigerator to help you.

In the book *Radical Acceptance: Embracing Your Life with the Heart of a Buddha,* Tara Brach (2003, 207) says, "Feeling compassion for ourselves in no way releases us from responsibility for our actions. Rather, it releases us from the self-hatred that prevents us from responding to our life with clarity and balance."

You Matter

The following are some ways to develop self-compassion. Check off the ones that resonate with you, and write down your own.

☐ Do a survey of your body. Notice where you are holding tension. Sit, stand, or lie down in a comfortable position. Take a few easy breaths and bring your attention to a part of your body that feels tense. You can breathe into the place of tension or send love to that part of your body. Don't work hard at making the tension go away. As you bring your gentle attention to your body, any suffering you are feeling may diminish. Feel what you are feeling with loving kindness and without judgment.

Here's an example: I direct my breath into my shoulders now because I feel the tension there from writing. I start to criticize myself because I haven't been sitting in an ergonomic way. I notice how tight my shoulders are. I'm reminded how I forget to lower my shoulders while I write, then I notice my fatigue. After a few more breaths I begin to feel grateful for the tree outside my window. I breathe, noticing the tree and a bird sitting on a branch. The negative thoughts stop, and then I'm drawn to rub my shoulders and gently stretch.

☐ Give yourself a hug, a kiss on the hand, or a pat on the back. Try this when you're being self-critical or when you just need some loving attention. Add some words like "I'm good" or "I'm doing my best," or "Now, now, honey, be nice to yourself!" Say something that sounds caring to you.

☐ Care for your body. Take a walk, do stretches, dance, run, take a bath, get a massage, or rest. Keep in mind that you deserve to care for your body, especially when you are under stress or being hard on yourself.

☐ A parent of twins told me that when things got tense, she had a spa night at her house after the kids were asleep with a bubble bath, candles, and a glass of wine. For you, being kind to yourself may mean putting a date night on the calendar for cuddling or sex. If you are a single parent, think about the last time you had fun with a friend.

☐ Listen to music that lifts your spirit. Music is a great way to change your mood. Find music that makes you happy or has a message you want to hear. Make a playlist that is specific to being kind to yourself.

☐ Accept your feelings. You can do this in the same way you might with a child who is being self-critical. You might say to your child, "Honey, I know you're feeling angry that you couldn't do the puzzle. It's okay to feel bad. I know you'll try again when you're ready. You work really hard at learning new things." Use kind words like these when you're being harsh on yourself. "I lost it. I was frustrated and didn't catch myself. I apologized and calmed down. I'll get a good night's sleep. Tomorrow's a new day." If it helps, address yourself as "you."

☐ Drink tea and eat something healthy. Use teatime as a reminder to be compassionate toward yourself. When I make myself tea, it feels like a gift. If you're a coffee drinker, make a cup and sip it slowly as you come back to yourself. Notice what foods give you energy and which ones make you feel groggy or bloated. Focus on things that are good for you, and remind yourself you deserve them.

☐ Laugh. A sense of humor goes a long way in reducing stress and suffering, and increasing good feelings. Watch or listen to something funny, laugh at yourself, or find someone to have a belly laugh with. You can start to laugh in a way that feels false, and soon it will turn into real laughter. Do a web search for "laughing yoga," and you can have instant company.

☐ Keep a journal. Write down a few things each day that you are grateful for. Include something that you like or appreciate about yourself.

☐ How do you express or develop kindness toward yourself?

_____

☐ What would you like to do when you're feeling self-critical that is new for you?

_____

For more information and to do a self-compassion test, visit Kristin Neff's website (http://www.self-compassion.org). For a more in-depth study of the pathways to self-compassion, read *The Mindful Path to Self-Compassion* (Germer 2009).

Value yourself. Raising a child is a difficult job.

A Thought to Consider:
Tracking might take some of the charge out of my reactions.

As you track for the next week or two, you will come to understand your yelling patterns. They will be less of a mystery, and you won't be so surprised by your child's behavior. The specific issues will become clearer, and your curiosity and efforts will reduce your reactivity. If you track your yelling throughout the day, you will be more prepared for trigger events.

Tracking will help you to be more responsive, especially if you deepen your ability to be compassionate toward yourself. Think of self-compassion as a win-win for everyone at home. It's a way to quiet the storm within, and you'll be more likely to connect with your child.

Chapter 6

"What Can I Do Instead of Yelling?"

Shifting Gears One Step at a Time

"Some days I feel prepared to deal with my rambunctious kids. When I don't automatically yell at them, I feel a whole lot better about myself. When I catch my anger before it builds, I can see them as children I love and not as enemies."

—Paul, father of children ages three, five, and eight

Calming your own state of mind is at the core of communicating with your children with love and respect. Yelling comes easily, and at first it can be difficult to remember to stop and pay attention to what's going on for you and your child. Persevere! With practice, you will be able to sense what you are feeling as you feel it, help yourself to think new thoughts, shift gears, calm yourself, and discover ways to help your child with the complexities of living and learning. Like most things you have accomplished that you are proud of, motivation and practice are essential.

Remember: your child is not the enemy. Your child needs attention, comfort, limits, guidance, reassurance, a gentle touch, and opportunities to succeed. And, like you, your child needs lots of time to practice the skills he or she is learning every day.

Thinking Differently About Discipline

Have you ever heard someone say, "That child is spoiled and just needs some good old-fashioned discipline?" Chances are, yelling or corporal punishment is what he or she had in mind. But you don't have to yell or use harsh punishment to teach your child right from wrong. Discipline is not synonymous with inflicting pain and suffering. Children do not benefit from being shamed, frightened, or rejected. But these forms of discipline are passed on from generation to generation unless the cycle is broken through awareness, conscious effort, and support.

There are many definitions of "discipline" in the dictionary. The definitions that I am most in agreement with are "To train by instruction and exercise, a branch of learning or instruction" and "instructions given to a disciple."

The word *disciple* (in a nonreligious sense) means that your child is your pupil and you are her teacher. Teaching, not retribution or punishment, is at the core of providing discipline.

Your job as a parent is to teach your child many things: to get along with and respect other people, to follow the family rules, to explore the world safely, to be kind and generous, and to develop healthy habits that will serve her well throughout life. Take a minute to think about the values you wish to teach your child. Are they the same as the values you grew up with?

Your child is more likely to cooperate with your requests and guidance if he senses you are on his side, with his best interests in mind. On the other hand, there will be times when your child will get angry at you for setting limits, cry when he thinks you are being unfair, or fuss at your rules. These are normal reactions as children discover that they are not the center of the universe and that they have to learn to live with certain rules of the family and society. When you discipline with love, even when you are firm, you will avoid using your authority for revenge, to vent your anger, or to humiliate.

In my work with parents, I have found that the concepts you will read about in this chapter the A-B-C-D-Es of Not Yelling and the 4 Cs of Discipline—are easy to understand and implement. With practice, your discipline style will begin to change, your stress will go down, and you will feel more at ease with your children.

The A-B-C-D-Es of Not Yelling

It is one thing to decide you are not going to yell at your child anymore, but it's quite another to learn to react differently when your yelling is triggered. The moment you feel triggered by your child, you can start taking the following five steps:

1. Ask

2. Breathe

3. Calm yourself

4. Decide what your child needs

5. Empathize

Ask

- What am I feeling?
- What are my escalating thoughts?
- Can I accept my feelings and reframe my thoughts?

Breathe

- As you ask yourself these questions, become aware of your breath.
- Breathe from your belly, and focus on taking three to five slow, easy breaths. You may want to count to four as you inhale and as you exhale. Sense your body as you breathe, and imagine every cell filling with oxygen. The main point is to bring gentle awareness to your breath.

- If your child is not in any immediate danger, take the time you need to focus on your breath before you respond.

Calm Yourself

- Focusing on your breath helps you regulate your emotions.
- By replacing your escalating thoughts with positive or realistic thoughts, you will calm your mind.
- The goal is to wait until you have calmed down before you discipline or communicate with your child.

Decide What Your Child Needs

- Think about your child's temperament and age. Do you have realistic expectations for your child?
- Does he need a consequence, a hug, redirection, encouragement, or a clear boundary?
- What meaning is his behavior communicating to you?

Empathize

- Put yourself in your child's shoes and try to sense what your child is feeling and thinking. Listen to what she says.
- Say something that communicates you understand what she might be dealing with or feeling.
- Now you can better decide what she needs.

The A-B-D-C-Es in Practice

The steps to not yelling are listed as A, B, C, D, and E to help you remember them, but you may not always want to do them in this specific order. For example, you may need to focus on your breath before you can ask yourself what you are feeling and thinking. Don't expect to remember all of the steps at first, just start. The rest will begin to come naturally as you practice.

The story that follows illustrates how Eva used the five steps on the nonyelling path when her daughter's crying triggered her anger.

• Eva's Story

Eva is a single mom. Five-year-old Molly lives with her every other week. They share the house with a roommate, Jackie, who sometimes watches Molly.

As a regular early morning weekend routine, Molly watches her favorite TV shows while Mom gets to sleep in. One morning around 9 a.m. Jackie asks Molly to turn the TV off because she is trying to work, and she thinks Molly has watched enough cartoons already. Molly immediately starts crying.

From the bedroom, Eva hears Molly crying and Jackie getting frustrated and talking loudly. As Eva pulls her blanket over her head, she asks herself, "What am I feeling?" She's feeling a lot: embarrassed that her daughter is being difficult, annoyed that her roommate isn't being more understanding, and angry that she has to get up and deal with this situation. She notices the tension in her shoulders and neck building.

Eva also becomes aware of her escalating thoughts, which involve judgment of everyone in the situation: *If Jackie were a parent, she would understand how hard it is to raise a kid. If I were a better mother, I would be up already with Molly since I don't see her every weekend. I wish Molly wasn't such a crybaby. She is such a drama queen. She is probably crying just to wake me up. She's just like her dad.*

Eva has been working hard learning how to yell less. She's getting better at becoming aware of her thoughts and then reframing them. So she chooses to stop her negative thoughts and calm herself: *We all need some space to do our thing this morning. Molly is a sensitive child. Making the transition to my house is always a little rough for her. Jackie has to work all weekend; no wonder she's stressed.*

Eva notices her breathing and takes a few easy belly breaths to put herself in a calmer frame of mind before she rushes out to save the day. Suddenly, she is aware of how much she has changed. In the past she would have jumped out of bed and yelled at her daughter, even if it was Jackie she was angry with. But now she can take a minute to collect herself and realize this is not an emergency.

When she goes into the living room she sits on the couch next to her daughter, who is still crying. She puts her arm around Molly and says, "Good morning! I bet you were enjoying your cartoons. Which one was your favorite this morning?" Molly's crying turns into a whimper as she tells her mother she wasn't finished watching and Jackie was being mean to her. Eva listens with compassion. Then, Eva turns her attention to Jackie and says, "Looks like you have to work on a beautiful Saturday morning. It must be hard to work with the TV on and me still in bed."

She doesn't try to quickly fix the situation. She uses her calm state to help the others reduce their intensity. She has learned that emotions are contagious, so she speaks softly and notices that Molly continues to calm down and Jackie is beginning to relax.

She gently strokes Molly's hair, something Molly really likes. After a minute or two Eva asks Molly if she's hungry and if she wants to help her make some yummy eggs and sausages for breakfast. Molly whines a little about her show, but agrees to go off with Mom. Jackie tells Eva that she is planning to go to the office soon and will be out of everyone's space.

Nothing more is really needed right then. Eva plans on having a talk with Jackie later tonight. She will remind her about how important it is for Molly to have warnings when she needs to turn off the TV, since she is slow to adapt and also quite strong willed. Jackie enjoys Molly, but often forgets to consider Molly's temperament and sometimes throws multiple commands Molly's way. Eva used to be embarrassed about Molly's sensitive, intense, and strong-willed nature, but she's getting much better at accepting her daughter for who she is. At the same time, she is also learning to set limits and not give in when Molly cries.

Eva suggests that the three of them have a household meeting on Sunday. They can plan a fun date for Jackie and Molly and clarify the rules about weekend TV watching.

Eva's Nonyelling A-B-C-D-E Steps

Here's how Eva used the steps in dealing with Molly and Jackie.

Ask: When she asks herself how she is feeling, she senses her anger, embarrassment, and tension. Molly's crying is a key trigger for Eva. She is able to hear and then reframe her negative thoughts to more reasonable and compassionate thoughts. When Eva cried as a child, she was yelled at and told to stop, or her mother would give her something to cry about. Eva knows to take time to sort things out in her own mind before stepping in.

Breathe: She takes a few slow belly breaths. She has practiced doing this at work and in the morning when she first gets up. She can feel her neck and shoulders begin to relax as she brings her breath and attention to them.

Calm: She waits till she feels calm, reminding herself that this isn't an emergency, and although her daughter is sad, she is safe.

Decide: She decides that she won't undermine Jackie's authority by turning the TV back on. Molly needs to learn to follow requests from Jackie. Eva doesn't feel like Molly needs any consequences from her. Her plan is to redirect her, help her calm down, and move on. She looks forward to having a pleasant day with her daughter and understands that transitioning from Dad's house to Mom's house is often difficult.

Empathize: As Eva approaches, she feels empathetic toward Molly. Her instinct is to give Molly a hug and acknowledge how she might be feeling sad or mad. She is able to comfort her daughter in a way she never knew from her own mother. Eva also empathizes with Jackie, who is clearly stressed out. Redirecting Molly to the kitchen works well. Eva knows that her daughter often cries more when she is hungry. Molly doesn't always realize she is hungry until Eva mentions food or brings her something to eat.

As Eva has more and more nonyelling days, she becomes confident in her ability to manage her feelings and help her daughter do the same. She is beginning to understand her patterns and forgives herself when she backslides and her frustration gets the best of her. Molly is having an easier time than she did last year, after her parents got divorced. Everyone in the family has been getting help to learn how to get their needs met and to also respect the needs of others.

The 4 Cs of Discipline

Doing the A-B-C-D-E steps will help you step back and address the misbehavior or difficulty you are facing with a clear mind and open heart. Sometimes, of course, more than a hug or redirection is needed. That's where the 4 Cs of Discipline come in!

The 4 Cs are key components of respectful discipline:

Communication

Choices

Consequences

Connection

In combination with the A-B-C-D-E steps, the 4 Cs will help you stay focused on the problem at hand and the rules that need to be followed. Your child will learn how to make good choices and accept the consequences when mistakes are made. Instead of resorting to yelling or harsh punishment, you will provide discipline while staying connected with your child.

1. Communication

- Keep it short, specific, and simple
- Show and tell
- Use encouraging words and the power of "I" and "you"

2. Choices

- Keep them real and simple
- Don't ask for permission, okay?
- It's your choice

3. Consequences

- Develop family rules
- Adjust rules and consequences based on your child's needs and developmental stage
- Review the consequences
- Use consequences that hold children accountable for their behavior

4. Connection

- Have one-on-one time
- Be curious about your child's feelings
- Don't hold a grudge

---

1. Communication

Clear communication is vital when you want your child to stop doing something she is not supposed to or to start doing something you want her to do.

Keep It Short, Specific, and Simple

Short, specific statements are more effective than general requests. "Please stop throwing the sand" is better than "Johnny, be nice now."

If your child is doing a new negative behavior, explain why it's not acceptable but first give a clear message of what you expect. "Johnny, don't throw the sand. It can get in someone's eye and that would hurt." (This is much more effective than going on and on: "Johnny, you know it's not nice to throw sand. I've told you already that you shouldn't throw sand at the park. You wouldn't want your friend Jed to have to go to the doctors to clean his eye out, would you?" Johnny stopped listening before you were halfway through.)

Give one instruction at a time. Children will frequently forget what you have asked if you say too many things at once, such as "It's time to get dressed, make your bed, pack your bag, and eat breakfast now!" Instead, slow down, muster up your patience, and say something like, "It's time to get dressed now. While you get dressed, I'll start breakfast."

Show and Tell

Whenever possible, get down to your child's level so you can make eye contact. You want to be sure you have your child's attention, and you are less likely to yell if you are face-to-face. Get close and say, "Don't throw the sand, but you can dig a hole with the shovel." Take the shovel and demonstrate the fun he can have in the sand. If he is easily distracted, ask him to repeat your instructions to be sure he heard you, or ask him to show you how big a hole he can dig.

Do you ever feel like you're being watched? Well you are—day and night. Your child learns so much about how to be in the world by what you do. If you yell or curse at the driver in the car that is going too slow, your child learns about impatience. If you complain about relatives who are coming over for dinner, your child learns to talk about people in a negative way. If you express gratitude for a neighbor who helped you carry your packages, your child learns about kindness. You are your child's first teacher, and you are looked up to, even with all of your imperfections.

Use Encouraging Words

Encouragement is more than just words of praise. What you say indicates your underlying attitude toward your child. Keep in mind that your tone of voice, facial expressions, and posture express a great deal about how you feel as well.

Be specific in communicating behaviors you want to reinforce. Take the following statement: "Kelly, as soon as you are dressed, we can have breakfast. I liked how quickly you got dressed yesterday. It gave us time to read a story before school." This mom is inspiring her daughter to cooperate instead of nagging her. Your friendly manner will encourage and teach. "Shannon, it sounds like you've been practicing your guitar a lot these days. That last song sounded crisp and clear. How did you like it?"

All children (and adults as well) need encouragement to tackle the challenges of life. A child who frequently feels discouraged needs an extra dose of positive regard, support, and opportunities to succeed. Encouragement can provide your child the sunlight she needs to bloom.

The Power of "I" and "You"

When you start a sentence with "I," you communicate what you feel about a specific behavior or action. Next you can ask for what you need. "I am getting a headache because it's too loud in here. I am glad you're having fun, but please go outside with this game." Or, "I am feeling angry because you keep ignoring me. Let's sit down at the table, finish our breakfast, and discuss what time we need to leave for your party. How are you feeling about going to Seth's house?"

The formula here is "I feel X when you do Y, so please do Z instead." You can practice this with your kids, spouse, partner, or even coworkers. At first it might feel awkward, but you'll see once you practice, it's a powerful way to communicate. It helps you identify what you're feeling and figure out what you need, and it can help you understand what's going on for your child.

Using the "I" and "you" approach will help you teach your child about emotions, so he too can communicate based on what he feels and what he needs. "Mommy, I'm so mad that Jed knocked my building down. I need someplace where he can't come." This expression of frustration is much better for everyone than "Jed is such a stupid jerk!"

I learned to stop asking my husband, "Why are you so oblivious?" and instead say, "I get angry when the kids are crying or fighting and you don't seem to hear them. I would appreciate it if you would step in to help." Changing my way of talking to him was important for our relationship.

It's a virtuous goal to eliminate all negative name-calling from your vocabulary. Name-calling is usually a trigger for someone else's anger. The power of "I" and "you" will help to prevent name-calling and yelling.

2. Choices

A child who feels like he has power and control in his life is a child who is less likely to fight, stomp, cry, or make demands for power and control. Offering choices, when it's appropriate, will reduce yelling and power struggles, and strengthen your child's decision-making skills. It will also help to support your child's sense that what he does and wants is important and that he matters.

Keep It Real

Many parents report giving choices to young children in this way: They pick out two shirts and say to their child, "It's time to get dressed. Decide which shirt you would like to wear today, the green one or the purple one." Or, "Do you want to take your bath now or after dinner?" In this case the child doesn't have a choice of bath or no bath, but having some say over when the event will take place can help a reluctant bather.

Be sure to offer a choice only if you mean what you say, and you truly intend to give your child a choice. It doesn't make sense to say, "You have a choice: get in your car seat right now, or I'm going to take off with you on the floor where it's not safe." Or, "You have a choice: you leave the park now with me, or I'll leave without you." These are not safe choices to give to your child. They are empty threats that you wouldn't follow through on and will probably lead to yelling when your child reacts with defiance. Children really want to know that they can trust you, so keep it real.

If your sensitive daughter wants to wear the same leggings every day because they feel comfortable, why not let her? If you can wash them when needed or buy a few pairs of the same leggings, then she gets a chance to develop her style and feel comfortable. Pick your battles.

Keep It Simple

Some parents fall into the trap of thinking that everything should be a choice. This isn't realistic. Even though you want your child to feel like she has power and decision-making capabilities, you still need to be the one making many decisions based on what you think is best.

Giving too many choices is overwhelming. You're bound to feel like a short-order cook at a restaurant if you ask your child, "Would you like a sausage, chicken, or a hamburger for dinner tonight? Or if you want I can make pasta instead."

A simple choice would be "We have blueberries or strawberries for dessert. Which would you like?"

Older children can work with you to problem solve situations that historically have turned into yelling matches. Give your teen some choice about when he'll do his homework and when he'll play on the computer. Together you can work out a plan. Then, it's your job to follow up to see that the plan is implemented.

Your children will be learning about the choices they make and the consequences they face on a daily basis. If the results of their choices are not what they had hoped for, help your children review their choices and think about what they would do differently.

Don't Ask for Permission, Okay?

Listen to what you say to your child and see if you have the "Okay?" habit. Parents sometimes add the word *Okay?* to the end of many of their sentences. If you do, now is a good time to stop. Many things that you say to your child don't involve a choice, so why ask for permission from a runny-nosed two-year-old? "Honey, it's time to blow your nose, okay?" or "Mommy will be gone for just an hour, okay?"

I have to admit that I automatically said "Okay?" sometimes. When I became aware of it, I realized I was undermining my own authority. Once I heard my wishy-washy style and noticed that it was not effective, I stopped. As a result, I felt more like an adult with appropriate, calm authority, especially when there really wasn't a choice.

It's Your Choice

How you respond to your child is always up to you. No matter how you respond, you are modeling behavior that your child—for better or for worse—is learning.

It's your choice, so think about the consequences of your choices: What are you teaching your child?

3. Consequences

Sometimes your child will accept clear communication from you and make good choices. At other times your child will test your limits or requests with whining, crying, pleading, or defiance. Some children take a long time to learn what is expected and what will happen if they don't listen to their parents or teachers. Remember that a child's temperament will impact his ability to follow your requests. For example, children who are slow to adapt will take longer, and intense children will protest louder.

You may often yell when things don't go as you expect or wish, and you don't know what to do instead. It's really okay to not know. Take a moment to stop, breathe, and consider what is needed. As you work to yell less, experiment with giving your child respectful consequences for unacceptable behavior. You'll learn by your mistakes and successes.

Consequences are a part of life, for kids and for adults. If your parking meter runs out of time and a parking enforcement officer drives by, you'll get a ticket. Not putting enough money in the meter or not moving your car has a consequence. You might be the type of person who likes to push the limits and hope for the best, but your luck may run out. There is a good chance you will remember to put enough money in the meter next time, because you don't like the consequence of spending your hard-earned money on a ticket. You know the rules, and you have choices about how you will follow them.

Say your daughter decides not to do her math homework for a few days. When you find out about it from the teacher, you tell your daughter that she has to complete her work on Friday night instead of going to the movies with a friend, because you have a family rule that all homework has to be completed before weekend fun. Her need to finish her work was reinforced by the consequence, and no yelling was needed. She begged you to let her go, but you stuck to the rule, reminding her that tomorrow was another day.

Develop Family Rules

A cornerstone of discipline and providing consequences for behavior is establishing family rules and expectations with your child. There will be much less resistance to the consequences you put forth if your child understands the rules. You can start this at a very early age and adjust as your children grow.

Babies Need to Know Their Boundaries

When your adorable nine-month-old crawls over to the cat food bowl for a morning snack, you can clearly let her know that she can't eat the cat food. You reinforce that concept every time she heads for the bowl. You redirect her, pick her up, and with a calm but firm voice let her know that it's not okay to snack on the cat's food. When you offer her some cereal, you remind her that she eats people food in her highchair. If your child is strong willed, chances are you'll repeat this process many times, until she learns. And if she is highly persistent, you may decide to move the cat food out of reach.

In this way, at a young age your child is introduced to a rule that she will later come to understand.

Three-Year-Olds Test the Rules

Mimi makes a picture chart for three-year-old Dash, so that he will know what he has to do before bedtime. Dash doesn't like to brush his teeth, but he is learning the rule that teeth are brushed before story time. Mimi shows Dash the picture chart and tells him it's time to brush his teeth. He usually cooperates, but one night when he refuses, Mimi reminds him that he can't have a story unless he brushes his teeth. When he refuses, she says, "I'm sorry you won't brush your teeth, but if you don't, there won't be a story tonight." Mimi sticks to the rule, even when Dash cries for a story. She doesn't change her mind. Without yelling, she gives him a hug and kiss, and she reminds him of the rule and that tomorrow night will be another chance to get a story. Mimi will also replace the battery on his electric toothbrush to make the bedtime teeth-brushing routine more fun.

Teenagers Push to Adapt the Rules

Zuzu doesn't like her 11 p.m. curfew on the weekends. She knows that if she is more than fifteen minutes late, she will have to come home an hour earlier the next night she goes out. If she doesn't call to say she'll be late, then she has her phone privileges taken away for a day. When Zuzu's lateness becomes a pattern, her parents talk with her about what's going on and pull in the reins until she is able to follow the rules again. She gets an earlier curfew until her parents can trust her.

Since her parents have stopped yelling at her (most of the time), Zuzu feels like she can talk to them about rules during a family meeting. Zuzu proposes a later curfew since all of her friends can stay out till midnight. She reminds her parents that she's been doing well in school and helps out with her little sister on the weekends. Her parents say they will think about it and consider a change, once she shows them she can follow the current rules for the next two weekends.

"I Will Consider It"

Rules and consequences can be changed as needed. They are based on your particular child and what he or she needs during a certain developmental stage. Don't change the rules just because your persistent teen has worn you down. You can always fall back on the statement "I will consider it" to give yourself some time to think.

Follow your gut when it comes to issues of safety, and talk with friends or relatives to get feedback when you're unsure of what makes sense. Remember that your teenager will be out of the house before you know it and needs your support to make good choices and learn from the consequences when she doesn't.

Review the Consequences

Many parents find it helpful to have family meetings as a child gets older. It's an effective way to present rules and consequences and get input and agreement so everyone will know what is expected. If you engage your children in rule making, there is a greater chance that they will follow them. I offer family meeting tips in chapter 7.

It's important to review with your child the consequences that will follow when rules are broken. You can't review every possible situation and consequence, but having some basic rules that you post for all to see will reduce yelling and arguments.

When your children don't follow a rule, remind them what the rule is, and whenever possible, give them a chance to comply. "Carrie and Jack, please stop arguing about the TV now. If you continue to argue, the TV will be turned off for the night. You know that's the rule, so I hope you can make a good choice."

Consequences That Are Related to the Behavior

Consequences can hold children accountable for their behavior and keep you from yelling. It's important that the consequences be related to the behavior that you want to teach your child. Children have "is it fair?" meters built in, so when they know the consequences, and they still choose to do the unacceptable behavior, on some level they get that it's fair.

Use Nonrescuing Consequences

Nonrescuing consequences are easy to do. But they can be oh-so-challenging for parents who are used to helping their kids out, no matter what.

When my daughter Carina forgot her lunch box the first time, I was happy to walk to school and take it to her. The second time, I wasn't happy about it, but I took time to deliver it. After that I realized that she would be more likely to remember her lunch box if I didn't deliver it to school. I stopped rescuing, and she started to remember.

Life provides all of us with many opportunities to learn from our experiences, and as a parent sometimes you just need to step back and not interfere. There was no need to yell at my daughter or make her feel bad for forgetting. Her need to ask friends for food was a consequence she learned from. I had warned her ahead of time that I wouldn't be bringing her lunch box to school again, so she wasn't surprised. These kinds of consequences are often referred to as *natural consequences.*

Of course, if a baby were about to touch a hot stove, you wouldn't let her learn about hot stoves by burning herself. You would intervene and stop her, since your job is to keep your child safe, as best you can.

Use Consequences That Make Sense

Every day, you teach your child many things, and if you want to yell less, logical consequences are frequently needed.

For example, Jason learned how to deal with Sasha and her cereal throwing without yelling. When Sasha throws her cereal on the floor, Jason reminds her of the rule. He shows her that cereal goes on her spoon and then in her mouth. He even encourages her by telling her how good she is getting at feeding herself, and he lets her feed him as well. As she starts to play with her food, he reminds her that if she throws the cereal, she will be taken out of her high chair. She happily feeds herself, but as Jason walks away to get his coffee, she throws the food on the floor (a game she likes to play). Instead of yelling the way he used to, he calmly takes her out of the high chair and firmly tells her that it's not okay to throw food. If he thinks she still needs to eat, he will try putting her back in her chair in a few minutes to see if the consequence helped her learn the rule.

If your child spills his juice, don't yell at him. Get a towel and have him clean it up. If he's young, clean it with him. If your child is kicking her soccer ball in the house, and you ask her to stop but she doesn't, give her a warning first. Then, if she continues playing, take the ball away. She knows the rules, and the consequence will help her remember them. You might let her have the ball back later, but only if she goes outside with it and keeps it in the garage.

Do your best to keep the consequences focused on a solution: the juice needs cleaning up; the ball makes marks on the walls so it needs to be played with outside. These are often called *logical consequences*.

Sometimes You Can't Think Logically

Jenna cursed at her mother, Maria, when Maria refused to buy Jenna a new pair of shoes. Maria was really angry and didn't know how to give a consequence that made sense. Maria needed to teach Jenna not to be disrespectful. She knew she wouldn't punish her daughter the way her parents would have—by washing her mouth out with soap.

Maria remembered a concept she learned in a parenting class: that children need to be taught that they have both privileges and responsibilities. Instead of yelling, Maria told Jenna that she was angry and that they both needed to cool off before they spoke. She asked Jenna to think about what she just did and why it was unacceptable. Maria said she would be back soon to talk about consequences.

Once Maria comforted herself and cooled off, she went to Jenna's room and told her that being disrespectful by saying a curse word was not allowed in their family. She asked Jenna why she was so angry, and she listened to her feelings of wanting to be like the other kids who had cool shoes. Then, she told Jenna that her cell phone privileges would be taken away for at least two days. Once she saw that Jenna could speak in a respectful way, she would get her phone back. Jenna was not happy, but she kept her thoughts to herself.

Later they brainstormed ways Jenna could earn extra money to pay for the shoes she wanted.

4. Connection

At the core of discipline is connection. Your child is more likely to cooperate with your requests if he feels connected to you and knows he is the apple of your eye. Even if you are a full-time working parent, it is essential to schedule time and find ways to let your child know that he is cherished.

One-on-One Time

Carving out time to give your child your full attention is an important part of a discipline plan. Your child may still challenge or defy you, but it will be even more challenging if you don't maintain a loving connection.

If you read other books for parents, you will discover varied terms for this highly respected strategy that many parenting experts recommend. Stanley Greenspan (1996), in the book *The Challenging Child*, calls one-on-one time "floor time." In their book *Positive Discipline A–Z,* Jane Nelsen. Lynn Lott, and H. Stephen Glenn (2007) call it "special time." Russell Barkley (2000) also refers to "special time" in his book, *Taking Charge of ADHD*. He says it is a way to use play and parental attention to develop and reward a child's appropriate behavior.

In my experience working with parents, introducing one-on-one playtime on a regular basis helps shift difficult patterns such as power struggles, sibling fighting, tantrums, and parental anger. Here are some key elements to this effective approach to connecting more with your child and yelling less.

Make a Date

Set aside time for you and your child to be together. Whether you call it floor time, special time, or one-on-one time, the idea is to let your child know that you would like to spend some time just with her. Many parents find this challenging because of their busy schedules, but it can be done, and it will mean a great deal to your child.

Even if you feel like you have plenty of time with your child driving in the car or reading bedtime stories, this is different. Your scheduled special time will allow for fresh ideas, new ways of being together, and a deeper appreciation for your child.

I suggest you plan for *at least* fifteen to twenty minutes together two or three times a week. You can of course do more, and for some of you, once a week is all you can manage with each child. Start where you can, and increase the frequency of one-on-one time gradually. If you can only do one-on-one time once a week, you might want to spend a longer time together. If you have more than one child, and you have a opouse or partner, divide and conquer. Each of you can plan for time with one child, and then the next week, switch which child you spend time with. Having a calendar or whiteboard really helps keep things straight, and it's a good way for the kids to be able to see when their time with you is coming up.

When my daughter Carina was a preteen and I was working a lot, I used to take her out for breakfast. It was a special way we could have one-on-one time together. She got to choose what she wanted for breakfast, and I loved having time to talk with her. We looked forward to our breakfasts together.

Follow Your Child's Lead

This is the tricky part for some parents. You may be used to making suggestions about the kind of play you want to do. During one-on-one time, let your child know he gets to choose what activity you do or game you play. I suggest no TV, video games, or computer time, but if you do allow computer games, have it be interactive. Your child may want to teach you something new. The idea is that you play something your child wants to play, and you participate, but in a more passive way than you might ordinarily do. For example, if your daughter loves to play with puppets, let her decide on the game and story line. Watch her, follow her lead, and do your best to engage your imagination along with hers, without telling her what to do. Your job is to relax, be curious, and become familiar with your child's play.

Another example is if your son wants to go outside on his scooter, walk along and let him decide which direction to go. Engage in conversation about what you see around you, and respond to what he wants to talk about. You might also be together in silence if that's what he wants. Your child might not want the special time to be over, so it's a good idea to set a timer if you need to limit the time you can spend together.

Multitasking Is Not Allowed

Put the laundry basket down, turn your electronic devices off or leave them in another room, and focus your full attention on your child and yourself. If someone calls, don't answer the phone, or if you can't resist, let the person know that you are unable to talk because you are having one-on-one time with your child. Your child will love hearing you say that.

Okay, I will admit that multitasking comes really easy for me. Years and years of being a nurse, with too many patients, taught me to make efficient use of my time. But professionals who study attention report that multitasking can lead to superficial learning. As Edward Hallowell (2006, 82) says in *CrazyBusy*, "For most people, multitasking is exciting, sometimes necessary, but rarely as efficient or effective as devoting your full attention to one task." Even though it's what we parents do, notice how it can be difficult to retain information and relax when you are doing many things at once. I would be a hypocrite if I told you never to multitask. Plus, I'm not sure it's even possible when you're raising kids. Just do your best to let it go during this one-on-one time with your child.

Look at your child with curiosity about who she is and how she thinks. Listen to her words as she weaves a story of dragons and knights. Don't instruct, advise, or lecture—instead be playful. I found this difficult to do, and I benefited greatly from practicing being present with my children and enjoying our time together.

Find Activities You Both Enjoy

One-on-one time is important with older children, but it's not always easy to come up with activities that you both enjoy. When my son Matt was thirteen, I was feeling distant from him, a bit like living with someone from another planet whose language and habits I didn't understand. Most of my communication was about what he should or shouldn't do, and the more I asked questions, the less he said. Following his suggestion, we bought a ping-pong table and put it in the living room. Yes, we really did that. My goal was to spend time with him a few times a week after school. I trained myself to keep my mouth zipped and just enjoy playing ping-pong. It worked really well, until he got too good at playing, and grew frustrated because I was too easy to beat. After that I enjoyed watching him and our other kids play together. I was able to appreciate Matt in a different way, which led to less frustration and yelling.

You may not have the space or money for a ping-pong table, but board games are also a terrific way to spend time with an older child. I have fond memories of hours playing board games with all of my children. As adults we still play Apples to Apples together now and then.

One-On-One Time Reduces Sibling Fighting

A certain amount of fighting and competition is normal among siblings. They are learning to resolve problems and get along with other children. A child may feel jealous of a sibling, especially if he thinks his parents pay more attention to the other child. Children often crave undivided attention from their parents.

One-on-one time is a valuable intervention at any age when there is sibling fighting. It helps to reduce resentment, and it helps a child feel important in your life.

Plan for time alone with each child, write it on a family calendar, and be sure to follow through. Each child will get individual time with you, and you will remember what you love about your children when you're not yelling at them to stop fighting.

Be Curious

When your child is upset and won't do what you've asked, one approach is to find out what's going on. If you are truly curious and can communicate your desire to understand more, your connection with your child will grow. You will also be able to solve problems that you didn't understand enough about before.

Your tone of voice is very important. If you say in an impatient tone, "Now just tell me what's going on here and why you aren't ready yet," your child will most likely reply with something like, "I don't know." If you are able to pay attention to your tone of voice and calm yourself first, your inquisitiveness will usually be welcomed. Your child will see that you listen, that you care about her feelings, and that you are willing to take the time to figure things out. "Angel, you look like you are feeling sad. Come sit on the couch with me and tell me what's going on in that cute head of yours." Curiosity has nothing to do with who is right and who is wrong. A curious approach to a problem may take time, but it is so much better for both of you to leave the house feeling connected instead of angry.

Don't Hold a Grudge

When your child does something that makes you steaming mad, how easy is it for you to let go of what happened and move on? Some parents are able to forgive their child's misbehavior, while others find that they hold a grudge and spend their precious time continuing to feel angry. When we hold on to anger, we are hurting ourselves and the people we love. Author and activist Anne Lamott (1999, 134) offers these words of wisdom in her book *Traveling Mercies*: "Not forgiving is like drinking rat poison and then waiting for the rat to die."

Many of us were never schooled in the concept of forgiveness. As parents we can learn how to forgive and then model it for our children. Forgiving does not mean that we agree with what another person did or forget what happened, but it does mean that we are willing to let it go, move on, and not disconnect from someone we care deeply about.

Donald Gets Stuck

Donald asked his twelve-year-old son, Miles, to help him clean up the basement on Saturday, which would include building new shelves. Usually, Miles likes working with his dad, but on this day he went off with his friends on a bike ride before Donald came back from the lumber store. Donald is furious when he sees Miles is gone because it's a two-person job and he wants to get it completed before his relatives come the next day.

Donald calls his son, but Miles doesn't answer. Finally, after many tries and much cursing, Donald is able to reach Miles. Miles explains that they rode much further than usual, and he didn't realize what time it was. "How can you be so irresponsible? Come home right now!" Donald makes it clear to his son that there will be a punishment for his actions. He expresses his anger in his tone of voice and overall hostility.

When Miles gets back, Donald yells at him again, grounds him for the night—and then tells him they still have to clean the basement.

They work together all afternoon in stony silence. It was an unpleasant day for both of them.

Miles was initially sorry for his mistake, but his dad wasn't able to let it go. As a result they both felt disconnected, and Miles wished he could just go into his room and be alone.

The lesson Donald was modeling for his son? Mistakes are not forgiven!

Donald's A-B-C-D-E Solution

Here are the A-B-C-D-E steps Donald could have taken to let go of his resentment, not yell, and not hold a grudge.

Ask: Donald recognizes his feelings of disappointment and hurt. He replaces the escalating thoughts that fuel his anger. *Miles is a self-centered, uncaring son* becomes *Miles is a good kid. He was excited to see his friends. Mistakes happen.*

Breathe: When Donald takes some slow belly breaths, he feels how tense he is about the upcoming visit from his relatives. He takes a few minutes to sit and sense what's going on for him. He remembers that he's always tense before people stay at the house, even though it usually turns out fine.

Calm: His breathing helps him calm down. He realizes that being angry all day will ruin the time with his son. Donald goes to the kitchen, turns on some music, and pours himself a cup of coffee as he waits for Miles to come home.

Decide: Donald will have a talk with Miles when he gets home. He will ask Miles why he thinks he forgot about their plans. When Miles comes home, he apologizes to his dad and offers to work into the evening if necessary. Donald decides that it really isn't as big a deal as he was making into be and that he won't punish Miles.

Empathize: Donald gives Miles a pat on the back, and they both agree that things have been hectic. Donald tells Miles that he accepts his apology and is happy to have his help. He also acknowledges that biking with friends is more fun than cleaning out the basement. They will work on it together until it's done.

The A-B-C-D-E approach provides Miles with both learning and connection. Spending the day working together will also be one of the many memories Miles has of the ways his dad taught him life skills as well as carpentry. This approach works because Miles just lost track of time. But if Miles were a boy who habitually forgot to show up, Donald might rethink his discipline and most likely use consequences to teach Miles about responsibility and commitment. When you take the time to think through a situation, you are being responsive to your child rather than reacting to a trigger or your own stress.

Be Reasonable and Respectful

As you learn to yell less and be kind to yourself more, it will become easier for you to be respectful toward your child, even when he is doing something to test your patience. Keep in mind that one of the goals of discipline is to teach your child self-control. If you keep this in mind, you will be more likely to manage and transform your negative reactions in order to be a good role model for your child.

Think about a boss or teacher you liked. How did that authority figure correct your mistakes or unacceptable behaviors? A good boss or teacher will give consequences in a respectful way, so you don't feel humiliated or discouraged. If you turn in a paper late, maybe you will get points taken off your grade. But if a teacher tells the class how she is disappointed in you for turning in your paper late, or she doesn't give you enough notice to finish the paper, your experience is quite different. A good boss or teacher has realistic expectations and carries out consequences in order to help you make better choices in the future, not to make you feel ashamed.

Consider your requests and what your child is capable of. If your nine-year-old is struggling with homework because he has trouble with reading, don't yell at him for not finishing in time for bed. He needs your help to complete a task that's challenging for him, not consequences. If he forgets to turn in his homework the next day, then there will be a natural consequence—he'll get points off of his score.

If your three-year-old gets frustrated putting her toys away, consider helping her get started instead of threatening to take them away from her. It's reasonable to teach her that the toys need to be put away before the next activity. A consequence might be that the paints and easel can't be set up until the toys are put away. If you help her get started, over time she will learn how to do it on her own. If you notice her mess is a trigger for you, change your escalating thoughts. Instead of thinking, *She's manipulating me and never listens to what I say*, you can remind yourself, *She's just three. It's normal to want to play instead of cleaning up. I can help her learn.* Not reacting from a place of anger will keep your discipline respectful and reasonable, and avoid a blowup.

In chapter 7 you'll learn more about how to repair your relationship when you yell and say things that are hurtful to your child. You'll also have a chance to review other ways to yell less, such as planning ahead, family meetings, and using a timer.

A Thought to Consider:
Discipline is different than I thought it was.

When your child's misbehavior is on the rise, listen, look, and reflect on what may be causing the conflicts or meltdowns. A child's misbehavior is often an expression of stress, fear, insecurity, or other emotions. Start by calming yourself, and then decide what your child needs.

Spend time with your child, and follow your curiosity to discover more about what makes him tick. Listen to your child and laugh along with him at play. Spending quality time together will be the glue that keeps you connected and reduces your yelling.

Raising a child takes time, attention, compassion, and patience—things most of you crave to have more of each day. Some days will be better than others. Keep going back to the A-B-C-D-E steps (ask, breathe, calm, decide, and empathize) to shift gears, and use the 4 Cs (communication, choices, consequences, and connection) of discipline. Your child is counting on you to be respectful, even when he makes mistakes.

Chapter 7

"Help, Another Storm Is Coming!"

Stay Calm, Make Repairs, and Plan Your Course

"I'm yelling less these days, but just as I begin to relax, my spirited daughter stirs things up with her sister. I wish we could have a few days of smooth sailing. I can't imagine what it will be like when they are both teens!"

—Lora, mother of nine- and eleven-year-old daughters

When I think about raising my four children, I'm struck by how much time, attention, and emotional energy I spent solving problems and figuring out what they needed. If you're like me, just when you feel like you're getting a handle on things—like managing tantrums or solving sleep issues—something new pops up. What worked last week doesn't work this week. There you are again, feeling uncertain, tired, and at times ready to throw in the towel. I learned to say to myself, "Tomorrow is another day" and "This too shall pass." You may have some quiet and harmonious days, but when you have a family, strong emotions and individual needs don't let up. It is just the way life is with kids, so adjust your expectations, notice the good stuff, and prepare for the storm.

In this chapter I'll present additional nonyelling tools, attitudes, and approaches for you to try out as you face new challenges. If you have stopped using the yelling tracker, consider going back to it for a few days. It will give you a fresh view on your triggers and escalating thoughts. Celebrate the successes you've had, and focus your attention on the times of day and situations that continue to set you off. Remember to keep the quality of your relationship with your child at the center of your discipline efforts.

Repairing the Past with an Apology

Saying you're sorry (and meaning it) can go a long way toward repairing your relationship with your child. Some parents are hesitant to apologize after they've lost it, because they think it makes them appear weak and without authority. The reverse is more likely, because apologizing takes strength and honesty. Your child will appreciate and respect your willingness to admit your mistakes and clear the air.

One reason it is so important to apologize is because you are your child's role model. When you say you are sorry, you teach your children the value of an apology and how to do it. They will have better relationships with family and friends if they can learn about empathy, responsibility, and forgiveness—three components of authentic apologies. An apology will also help your child heal from the hurt he feels after you've yelled, and you will feel a sense of relief as you reconnect with him.

Your children are watching you to learn how to treat others. If you apologize after you have yelled at your kids, it will be easier to teach your daughter to apologize to her brother after she has screamed at him for going into her art supplies and making a mess.

Forgive Yourself First

First, forgive yourself for your strong reaction. Take a few minutes to understand what set you off. Remind yourself of your goals, and remember that mistakes can be forgiven. It's okay to feel remorse and to think of what you could have done differently. It might be like this: *Wow, I was caught off guard just now. I forgot to have lunch, and I've taken my hunger and frustration out on my kids. I'm sorry I did that. It's not their fault that I forgot to take care of myself. I'll get a quick snack and then go apologize.* Be honest with yourself about the hurt you caused your child. You may have forgotten to have lunch, but that doesn't mean you need to yell. Once you accept responsibility in your own mind, you can forgive yourself for the transgression. You may not have received apologies from your own parents, so it's vital that you start to forgive yourself when you make mistakes. Being kind to yourself prepares you to be kind to your child.

Ingredients of a Sincere Apology

In the book *The Power of Apology*, Beverly Engel (2002) discusses the three Rs of an apology: regret, responsibility, and remedy.

Regret

If you yell at your child and hurt her feelings, it's natural to feel regret or sadness. You didn't want to hurt your child with your reaction, but since you did, expressing regret is a good next step. "I'm so sorry that I lost it this morning when I came into your bedroom. What a lousy way to start the day. I know that made you feel bad."

Responsibility

It's vital to take responsibility for your actions. "I'm sorry I hurt you by yelling and saying you're lazy. I know better than to call people I love names." It is *not* a sincere apology if you add this statement: "I just get frustrated when you don't do your weekly chores on time like you're supposed to." It's your job to take full responsibility for your actions without blaming the other person. He or she may choose to apologize as well, but that isn't the goal of your apology. If there is a behavior that is triggering you, like undone chores, there are approaches other than yelling or blame to address that behavior.

Remedy

As you work to repair your relationship, think about a specific way to remedy the hurt you caused by yelling. You want to let your child know that you will work hard to not repeat your reaction and do your best not to yell. After you have taken responsibility, you might add something such as, "I'm going to work even harder at not yelling. Let's go out for a snack after school so we can talk about your schedule and weekend plans."

Wait to apologize until you are no longer angry or frustrated. Don't say "Sorry" and not mean it. Often parents teach children to say a quick, empty "Sorry" for something they did, without helping them learn to empathize. It takes time and practice to teach children to be compassionate toward others.

If you are apologizing many times a day for yelling, your apologies will lose their meaning. If this happens, it's a sign that you need more support to stop your yelling habit. Check in with yourself to see if your stress level is rising, if you're not getting enough sleep, or if you're forgetting to meet your emotional needs. Talk to a friend, relative, or professional. Reread previous chapters of this book, think of the consequences of your actions, and remind yourself of why the goal of yelling less is so important to you.

Proactive Approaches to Yelling Less

There are innumerable ways to be proactive in your parenting, and you will discover many on your own. For now, begin by keeping these three main points in mind: *Think and plan ahead, communicate your plans, and maintain a positive attitude about the plans.* There will be times when getting your child's input on plans is a good idea and other times when it will just complicate matters.

Plan Ahead

Being proactive with your child means that you plan ahead in order to prevent power struggles and other challenges. You're not in the reactive "put out the fire" mode, but instead you are thinking about your schedule, what your child needs, and how to make your day go smoothly.

For example, before you go into the grocery store with your eight-year-old, have a talk about what you are shopping for. Give him a list of things he can find for you, and let him pick out his favorite fruit or one of the cereals on your acceptable cereal list. Remind him that begging for treats is not part of the trip, but he can pick out frozen yogurt to have after dinner, when the shopping is done. Ask him for ideas of healthy foods to have for snacks at home and for his lunch box. Communicate your expectations—*before* you start shopping—in a clear and friendly way to reduce begging and pleading.

When you plan, it's important to keep your child's temperament in mind. Going to a crowded grocery store at 5 p.m. with a child who is sensitive to noise and is hungry is a recipe for disaster.

Plan with Your Child's Temperament in Mind

Some planning-ahead strategies work for most children. For example, it helps to have a plan regarding how much screen time is allowed each day or what the bedtime ritual is. If you are consistent and communicate these rules, you will reduce conflict and yell less. If, in addition, you think about your child's temperament as you plan ahead, you are more likely to meet her needs and help her follow through with what you have asked of her.

Here are some examples of children with specific temperament traits and ways their parents yell less by planning ahead.

Slow Adapting and Energetic

Latoya is a slow adapting, energetic four-year-old. Once a week her mother Ruth needs to get to work early. On those days, Ruth gets up an hour ahead of her usual time, since she knows how difficult it can be to get her daughter to stop playing and get out of the house. Ruth showers, gets dressed, and has her coffee before she wakes up Latoya. The night before, Ruth lays out the outfit for the day and gets lunch packed. When Latoya wakes up they play a "get-dressed-fast" game. If Latoya can be dressed and have her hair combed in fifteen minutes, she gets a special breakfast of waffles, strawberries, and bacon. It's Latoya's favorite breakfast, and she's motivated to move fast and help her mom get it ready.

You might be tempted to call this breakfast a bribe, but I call it motivation. There are many mornings I would have rolled over and turned off the alarm if I wasn't being paid to go to my job. We often need external motivators when our internal drive is tired. It's important that not everything Ruth needs Latoya to do be motivated by a special meal or game. This fun ritual has become something Latoya looks forward to, in part, because she and Mom get to play this game together. And yes, she loves her waffles as well.

Sensitive and Slow to Warm Up

J. J. is a sensitive, slow-to-warm-up ten-year-old. Whenever there is swim practice after school, J. J. complains about something, like a headache or being tired. He tries to talk his father, Leo, into letting him skip practice, even though he really loves swimming and wants to be on the team.

Leo is frustrated by J. J.'s complaints, so he reaches out to the coach for suggestions. The coach thinks that J. J. would do better if he got to practice early to warm up. J. J. likes this idea, and Leo has discovered that there is less conflict if he gets his son to swim practice about twenty minutes before the other boys come. J. J. looks forward to practicing on his own when it's quiet and just his dad is watching. Leo gives him feedback and encouragement. J. J. is less resistant to going, and Leo has stopped yelling when it's time to get ready for swimming. A slow-to-warm up child often needs extra time and space to feel comfortable and confident.

Intense and Persistent

Amaya, an intense and persistent six-year-old, always interrupts her father, Cal, with a new idea or question. She won't let up until Cal yells. Cal finally found a solution: he has taught Amaya to use the voice recorder on his phone. When Cal needs a few minutes of quiet time after dinner, he sets the timer and Amaya knows she can record her questions and ideas instead of interrupting her dad.

Cal and Amaya listen to the recordings at bedtime, and they laugh and talk about her commentary and questions. Amaya looks forward to this time with her dad and has even started to record some original songs for him.

You can see how understanding temperament can inform your plans and help you deepen your empathy toward your child and his or her style of being in the world. When planning, think about your temperament as well and what you need to stay calm, in spite of all you have to do.

Use a Timer

Timers are wonderful for helping children know what to expect and when it's going to happen. And in addition to helping you manage your kids, timers can actually teach valuable lessons.

Children thrive on having limits that are fair and are communicated respectfully. A timer is a neutral object to help your child with transitions and taking turns. A child's crocodile tears can't manipulate a timer (as they can a parent) when it's time to stop an activity.

As children learn to control their impulses and understand the consequences of their actions, they feel good about themselves and their abilities. Being able to stop playing and clean up the toys can add to a child's sense of belonging to a family or to a school where there is order, not chaos.

Young children tend to like timers, but as children get older they may become more resistant. Timers work well with teens if you allow them to have input about the limits and plans.

Here are few examples of using the timer instead of yelling.

Taking Turns. One of your jobs is to teach socially acceptable behavior, such as taking turns. Letting someone else swing, when you're having so much fun, is not something that comes naturally to most children. The timer is a great help in teaching children to take turns, to keep track of time, and to be reassured that they will get their turn soon.

Here is an example of how to use a timer to manage a typical sibling argument.

Kathy: Tommy, you've been using the computer all day. It's my turn now.

Tommy: That's not true! I just got on it. Mom was using it before.

Kathy: You've already played your stupid game five times.

Tommy: I have not!

Mom: It looks like this is a job for the timer. Starting now, you will each have fifteen minutes to use the computer before dinner. When the timer dings, it's the other person's turn. If you need the computer to do your homework tonight, we'll talk and figure out how much time you each need. Since Tommy has already had a turn, Kathy, you can use the computer now for fifteen minutes.

Tommy: But Mom, I haven't used the computer for a whole fifteen minutes yet.

Kathy: You've been using it for an hour!

Mom: We're moving forward so you can both have a turn. Otherwise, we'll need to shut it off. I know it's hard to tell how long you've been on the computer unless you use a timer or look at the clock. I always lose track of time. Tommy, why don't you come into the kitchen while I get dinner ready?

Transitions. Difficult transitions may be announced by tantrums (your child) followed by yelling (you). Too often a transition means your child has to stop an enjoyable activity and start one that isn't as much fun. Such transitions include going from playtime to cleanup time, getting ready for bed, and preparing to leave the house. You can use the timer to signal the end of an activity as well as to signal the beginning of an activity.

Ending a Game. Children and adults often have different expectations when it comes to playing games, and it's easy for everyone to lose track of time. When there is a limited time available for playing a game (due to anything from impending bedtime to thinning parental patience), a timer can provide a clear ending point.

Here's an example.

Jenny: Mom, will you please play Monopoly with me, please, please?

Mom: I'd love to, Jenny, but Monopoly can last for hours, and you have to get ready for bed soon.

Jenny: Okay, how about we play and then leave the game set up so we can finish it tomorrow? Please.

Mom: Sure. Let's see, it's 7:15 now. We'll stop at 8:00. I'll set the timer so we can get you to bed on time.

It's 8:00 p.m., and the timer rings.

Mom: It's time to stop playing and get you ready for bed.

Jenny: But Mom, it's my turn now. Come on, let's just keep playing a little while longer.

Mom: I'll tell you what. You can throw the dice for a last turn, but that's it. (*Mom knows that Jenny needs to finish up with a last turn as part of her transition.*)

Jenny: Wow, I got a monopoly. I'll put up some hotels.

Mom: Jenny, you'll have to do that next time. It's time to stop playing, as we agreed. Why don't you write a note about what you want to do next, so you don't forget to buy hotels tomorrow? (*Mom knows that Jenny will keep pushing the limit if she lets her.*)

Jenny: Oh, okay, Mom. But you promise we can play tomorrow?

Mom: If you get all your work done by 7:15 and nothing unexpected comes up, we should be able to play again. (*Mom has learned to stay away from the word promise since things do change.*)

Getting Ready for Bed. Sean never wants to go to bed. Even when he's completely worn out, he hates to stop what he's doing to change into his pajamas, wash up, and brush his teeth. He is eight now, but he has been like this since he was a toddler. He really enjoys the bedtime stories his dad, Tim, makes up every night. Tim has explained that when he says it's time to get ready for bed, Sean has fifteen minutes to do so. Tim always sets the timer, and Sean knows that if he isn't ready by the time the timer goes off, Tim won't tell him a story.

Sometimes Sean gets caught up in his play, fusses about having to stop, and forgets to brush his teeth. When he misses the deadline, Tim tells him that the story will have to wait till tomorrow night. He kisses Sean goodnight and sits with him for a few minutes and talks about his day. Missing his dad's creative stories is usually enough to help Sean remember to be ready for bed when the timer rings.

Time to Settle Sibling Fighting. Most parents find it difficult to listen to their children arguing with each other. It drives many parents to scream, curse, or say things they later regret. Sibling spats were the main reason I yelled at my children. Many parenting experts recommend "letting the children work out their own problems," but all too often parents don't have the tolerance and patience that requires. Kids also need to be taught problem-solving skills and consideration for others. And, it is important that you be on the lookout for any physical or verbal abuse between children. Abusive treatment should always be stopped if you're around to notice or hear about it from one of your children.

One way to cope when your children (or their playmates or cousins) disagree is to give them a set time to work out their differences. If they can't resolve their conflicts, you decide on the consequences.

Here's Tommy and Kathy again with a familiar conflict.

Tommy: Give me that, you little brat! (*Tommy grabs his toy and gives his sister a little push.*)

Kathy: Mommy, Tommy pushed me!

Tommy: Mom, Kathy took my Transformer and didn't want to give it back!

Kathy: You weren't even playing with it—it was on the couch. I hate you, you never let me play with you and your dumb toys.

Mom: Okay, you two, you know the rule. You have five minutes to come up with a peaceful solution to this problem. No hitting, name-calling, or pushing is allowed. I'm going to set the timer. If you haven't stopped arguing by the time it rings, you'll have to separate and play by yourselves until dinner.

Tommy: Mom, that's not fair. Kathy started it!

Mom: Now it's time to move forward and come up with a plan about playing so you are both satisfied. I'll set the timer. (*Mom sets the timer for five minutes and leaves the room.*)

Ending A: After five minutes, the timer rings, and the kids continue to argue. Mom tells them they need to play in separate rooms until dinner. She says that they will all talk after dinner about what to do when Kathy wants to play with Tommy's toys and how to work it out without hurting each other.

Ending B: The timer rings, and the kids have worked out their difficulties, dropped the argument, and gone to the back yard to play ball. At dinnertime Mom gives them some positive attention for their efforts: "You did a good job working out your problems. There are many adults who have trouble doing what you just did. How did you do it?"

Timer Tips

These are suggestions for you to consider. Adapt them to your family's needs and temperaments.

- Have a timer readily available so that older children can use it themselves.

- The time you set for a turn will depend on the child's age and the type of activity—generally speaking, the younger the child, the shorter the time for each turn.

- If there is conflict over who goes first, flip a coin. Most kids will go along with it.

- Praise your children for using the timer correctly, especially if they've been able to use it on their own. By doing so, you are reinforcing acceptable ways to work out conflicts.

- If you give consequences for not following the agreed-upon rules, don't be too harsh. Children will learn their lessons with reasonable consequences.

- Establish a clear routine for dealing with arguments, and stick to the family rules.

- Don't take sides. You can ask if the kids need help solving a particular problem. Their ability to solve problems will depend on many factors, including age, temperament, training, and practice.

- If you are using the timer to end arguing and your kids request more time to work out their differences, use your judgment. It's fine to reset the timer and give them more time if it sounds like they are making progress.

- The timer can also remind you to take a few minutes to focus on your breathing, sense your body, notice what you're feeling, and think about what you need to stay calm and responsive. We all need a time-out from the busy pace we tend to get caught up in.

Schedule Family Meetings

There are many reasons to give family meetings a try as a part of your proactive approach to parenting. Regular family meetings can provide an opportunity to express family values, plan time together, clarify expectations, offer appreciation, and deal with concerns and challenges. The goal is for your family to feel like a team that wants to learn to work and play well together.

Challenges

Perhaps you feel uncertain about starting family meetings. Maybe you don't think you can get your kids or your partner to participate. For some people the idea of a family meeting seems too formal; for others, finding the time seems impossible. My husband and I had some challenges with family meetings when we first started—I can still hear my teens moaning when I told them it was time for a family meeting. Now, I wish we had started having family meetings when they were younger.

We made a lot of mistakes in the beginning. We let the meetings go on for too long. And we didn't realize that we should include more positive agenda items every week, such as expressing appreciation and planning outings. On the other hand, we did have some notable successes. One idea that came out of a family meeting was the "hurricane cleaning hour": a predetermined hour in which we would all work together to get the house in shape. We had a system to rotate tasks, put on music, and all pitch in.

Even though the meetings weren't always smooth, they were a way to communicate to our kids that their feelings and ideas were important to us and that we valued their participation.

Opportunities

Many parenting professionals agree that family meetings are valuable, but their approaches vary.

Family meetings should focus on solutions, not complaints. If you're trying to understand a problem, investigate the issue. Ask clarifying questions and make sure that the person who has a concern feels understood and listened to. For example, if your daughter tells you she doesn't want to do her chore of feeding the cat anymore, give her time to talk about what has changed. Ask the other children if they've had a similar experience. Together, brainstorm potential solutions. Perhaps someone else is willing to feed the cat. Your daughter may be ready to take on a more challenging chore.

The creative problem-solving and communication skills that your children learn by taking part in family meetings will be of value to them at school, at work, and with their friends. Many small problems can be worked out before they grow into big issues, and your children are likely to feel more competent.

Guidelines for Successful Family Meetings

Successful family meetings take practice, patience, and a positive attitude. The basic structure listed below is a good place to start. Use it to come up with a plan that works for you and your family. Experiment to find the right balance between solving problems and planning for fun. Start off small and positive so your kids will want to come back for more.

When: Pick a time that's best for your family. Every Sunday night after dinner might work; or Saturday morning, before everyone gets busy. Stick to the same day and time as much as possible, and keep the meeting short—twenty minutes is about right and is a relatively easy amount of time for everyone to carve out.

Where: Any place that's comfortable—dining room table, living room, den, or outside. Turn phones and electronics off, and find a place with few distractions.

Who: Children as young as four years old can participate, depending on their temperament and maturity. Younger children can play quietly while you meet if it's not too distracting. Most children like family meetings as long as there isn't yelling, arguing, comparing, or blaming. It's always best if the entire family participates. If one parent is away, you can still have the meeting. The parent who is traveling can send in an agenda item or can join the meeting by phone.

How:

- Print an agenda sheet where family members can note ideas or issues, and post it on the refrigerator or whiteboard during the week. Agenda items may include where to go on the weekend, chores to be done, planning a sleepover with friends, or a new system for getting the kids ready for school on time. Encourage everyone in the family to post their ideas or problems.

- Announce the date, place, and time of the meeting.

- Decide who will run the meeting. If it makes sense in your family to rotate the chair of the meeting, try it. Many kids enjoy learning how to run a meeting. Doing this will also help you move out of the authoritative role that you are probably in most of the time.

- If people in your family interrupt frequently or have trouble taking turns talking, use a "talking stick," or any item that you can hold in your hand. When it's your turn to talk, you hold the stick. When you are done, you pass it to the next person for their turn.

After: Write down agreements so they are not forgotten. Thank each person for his or her contribution. End on a high note.

Suggested Agenda for a Family Meeting

- Set a timer. This will help you stick to the agreed amount of time and end on a positive note. If you have older children and there is productive brainstorming and collaboration going on, when the timer goes off ask everyone if the meeting should be extended.

- Give feedback about what's working well in the family. A popular approach is to take turns saying one thing you appreciate about each family member. After a few weeks, teach your children to give specific examples of things the other person did that they appreciate. "I appreciate Peter's sense of humor. When I was feeling bad yesterday, he came into my room and told me silly jokes until I forgot about my knee hurting."

- Address children's concerns first. Kids will be more interested in cooperating when their issues are addressed. Prioritize the issues you want to tackle at the meeting. Don't take on too much. You can defer some things till next week.

- Include one parent concern per week. Just think, in a year you can cover fifty-two issues! If you have a partner or spouse, talk before the meeting so you can be on the same page in terms of priorities and positive framing of the issue.

- Brainstorm solutions. During brainstorming, no idea is censored (you may want to specify that violent ideas are not allowed). After brainstorming you can discuss which ideas seem doable. Agree to try an idea out for a week and evaluate it at the next meeting.

- Write down action items. Post them for all to see during the week.

- Review the family calendar for the upcoming week. This will help you all be prepared for rehearsals, sports practice, meetings, and special events.

- End with a plan for something fun in the near future (this may be a part of the brainstorming session). You can plan big activities, like going camping next month, and smaller activities, like a pizza-and-board-game night on the weekend. Having fun together as a family is a great way to reduce conflict and yelling.

- Serve a snack. Some families who meet after dinner save dessert for during or after the meeting. You can also make popcorn a regular, healthy family-meeting treat.

An Abundance of Nonyelling Approaches

An essential quality to cultivate as a parent is a willingness to be attentive and open to what is happening in the moment, with yourself and with your child. This simple and yet challenging mind-set is at the core of everything else I suggest in this book.

I have recommended innumerable tips and strategies to parents over the years and used them with my own children and grandchildren.

Some I learned by trial and error; others I learned from books, videos, and other professionals. Below are some of the most effective approaches and ideas from my forty-plus years of learning about child development and the complexities of parenting. The descriptions are brief, so if you are drawn to any of these ideas, you can find out more in the resource section of this book or by turning to the World Wide Web.

Use Routines, Charts, and Calendars

"I just couldn't get my child to stop dawdling in the morning and begging for computer time in the evening. I'm now doing a chart that helps with both. My morning yelling is a thing of the past. I hope it lasts!"

—Mel, father of a seven-year-old
computer wizard

Teachers know that children thrive on routine and predictability. Their school day would be chaotic without a plan. Children feel secure when they know what they can count on. Having structure can help children learn about boundaries, especially when they have freedom within that structure to explore.

For example, providing your child with an after-school schedule can help to eliminate begging for screen time or complaining about having to do homework. A simple chart on the wall or on a clipboard works wonders for most kids as they reorient after school. Sit with your school-age child and plan for the things that need to be done from 3:30 to 8:30 p.m. Together, you can decide if playtime will come before or after homework, and how long it will be. Build in some downtime after homework is finished and before it's time to get ready for bed. With routine and structure also comes flexibility when needed. Don't be afraid to change things as you evaluate what's working and what isn't.

If there are complicated schedules for many family members, a big whiteboard can be a lifesaver. You can have everyone's names listed in the vertical column and the days of the week in the horizontal one. On Sunday, chart your week together so there are no big surprises—for

149

example, you have a last-minute business trip, and suddenly there's no one to take your daughter to the school play.

Another way to use a chart is to list a few things that your child needs to do every day. For example, if your three-year-old gets distracted easily before bedtime, make a chart that has a picture of a child brushing his teeth, using the potty, and getting his pajamas on. The visual images will help keep him on track. You can have him move a clip or clothespin to each picture after it's done.

Some people use charts associated with privileges to motivate their children's behavior. There are pros and cons to this approach. I suggest you keep it simple, easy to track, and for a specific amount of time to change a behavior and accomplish your goal. For example, if you are always yelling because your child fusses in the morning, you can tell him that if he gets dressed, brushes his teeth, and has breakfast without a fuss by 8 a.m., he can earn a privilege, such as thirty minutes of screen time after school. Every day, put a check mark or star on the chart for each thing he does without a fuss. You can even divide them into ten-minute accomplishments—if he does one without complaining, he gets ten minutes of the privilege, two gets him twenty minutes, and three gets him all thirty minutes. Or you can set it up so that all three things need to be checked, otherwise no screen time for the day.

Using this approach can help your child work on specific behaviors and can help you break a yelling pattern. If you do this for a couple of weeks, chances are your child will be more cooperative in the morning, and then you can stop charting. Let your child know that you are pleased with the hard work he did changing his morning habits. Remind him that he can get his thirty minutes of screen time after dinner if he continues to get ready on time for school without fussing, and if he is having trouble, he can come to you for help. This is the privileges-and-responsibilities approach: "You can have your computer privileges if you are responsible and do what's needed in the morning." If you use a chart for too many things or too often, your child may expect that everything she does will have an external reward.

Teachers use behavioral charts for children who need extra motivation to follow the rules. There too, it's best if the chart is not used as a punishment, but as a way to track efforts toward a goal. Parents have also reported good success with sticker charts for kids who are learning to use the toilet. Putting a sticker on a chart can help a child feel proud of her efforts. If this approach interests you, do some research for further guidelines.

Lower Your Voice

A simple technique to try is to substitute yelling with a whisper. When your child hasn't followed your request to put her shoes on, walk over to her, stand quietly, and then whisper slowly, "Please put your shoes on." She will be surprised by your new approach, and you will capture her attention while staying calm. Some children will find it compelling a few times and then get bored with this new approach. Other children will enjoy the shift and like your calm voice. Either way, you can be clear and direct without yelling.

Use Humor, Surprise, and Creativity

Marjorie, the mother of a toddler, told me a funny story about how she got her daughter to stop having the "dreaded tantrum" in the aisle of the grocery store. As her child pounded the floor crying for candy, Marjorie got down next to her and started to pound and make funny noises as well. The child immediately stopped her tantrum—she was shocked at how funny her mommy looked on the ground. Marjorie didn't care what other people thought, and her good sense of humor helped her daughter regain her composure.

If your child is intense, humor and surprise are great substitutes for yelling. As your child loudly complains for the tenth time that the trip is taking too long and that he's tired of being in the car, pull the car over (if it's safe) and get him out to do fifty jumping jacks. Play a game of how you wish you could turn the car into a rocket ship to reach the sky, and then ask your child what he would turn the car into. Empathize with him about how long it is taking and then engage his imagination. Buy a CD of silly songs or jokes and have some good laughs together while you drive.

I still remember a mother who came to a class for parents of kids with attention deficit/hyperactivity disorder. She said the only thing that kept her from yelling and giving other harsh punishments was

151

playing a get-dressed-game with superhero puppets. Superman or Wonder Woman would help her son pick out his clothes and put them on. The stories this mother made up while her son was dressing helped him stay focused and not become distracted by all of his toys in his room. This mother was very clear that the early morning puppet show was worth it, since she and her son hated the yelling matches.

Try Counting

My friend Isabelle has three-year-old twins, and she has found that counting to three works like magic. She uses a simplified version of the popular 1-2-3 Magic time-out system that Thomas W. Phelan (2010) developed. She simply says, "Please stop playing now." And if they don't listen, she says in a calm but firm voice, "I'm going to count to three. It's time to leave." As soon as she says, "That's one," they start to scurry. Her kids seem to need the warning, and then they usually do what Isabelle says. I asked her what she does if they don't comply. She said she just insists by picking them up or doing something else that communicates that she means what she says. The key here is that the children know by her tone of voice and the words "I'm going to count" that their time is up, and they have to listen to Mama.

Wait It Out

If your child knows that she can't take the paints out until the other toys are put away, give her a reminder and time to comply. You can wait it out if you don't have to be somewhere. Just stick to what you have said, and see the choices your child makes. If she starts to whine about wanting to paint, you can sound like a broken record and just calmly say, "I'll get the paints down as soon as you put your animals away. Let me know when you're done." If you think the number of stuffed animals strewn around the living room overwhelms her, you can help her out, but be sure she is doing some of the work.

The key point is to not change your mind and clean up for her because she starts to whine. That is a sure way to encourage whining. The more consistent you are with "No painting until the toys are cleaned up," the sooner she will learn to do her part. The broken record approach I just described is a way to stick to what you want to see happen without losing your cool. You repeat your instructions so your child understands that you are sticking to your plan.

Pick Your Battles

Picking your battles is a common parenting strategy that points to the need to have realistic expectations of your child and to resist your perfectionist tendencies. As you know by now, the reality of a quiet, clean, and orderly home went out the window when the stork flew in. If you try and correct every little thing that your child does that you don't approve of, you will collapse from exhaustion and run the risk of making every interaction with your child a battle of wills.

Review your values. Think about the adult you hope your child will become some day and what she needs to learn to get there. Core values—such as honesty, kindness, and cooperation—can inform you about the battles that are worth fighting. If your two-year-old child hits you, address that behavior. If you ignore her behavior, she will learn that it's okay to hit people. You don't need to yell, but you do need to let her know, in no uncertain terms, that she may not hit you.

On the other hand, if your child wants to wear his Superman pajamas to the grocery store, is it really something to argue about? Or if your daughter's shirt and pants don't match, is it necessary to criticize her and make her change? Maybe you can save the exclamation "No way can you wear that outfit!" for going to a school event or a nice restaurant with relatives. Think about what really matters to you, and let the small things go.

If you know your slow-to-warm-up child needs time to feel comfortable in new situations, be prepared to pick your battles. For example, if you go to someone's house, and the kids are sitting at a separate table from the parents, what do you do if your four-year-old wants to be with you? Instead of arguing with him and telling him to be a big boy like the other kids, consider keeping him nearby until he's comfortable in this new environment and ready to move away from you. This is an example of how knowing his temperament will help you decide which battles to pick, even if someone else thinks you're being too "easy" on your cautious son.

"Let's Take That Over"

This is a simple approach to help your child learn acceptable behavior. Just as a movie director asks an actor to take a scene over again until he is satisfied, you can ask your child to "take two" or "take three" when needed. For example, politeness may be a core value for you, and when your child isn't polite, you get upset. Instead of yelling, "Stop being so rude," you can calmly say, "You know that it is important in our family to say 'please' if you want more food. Reaching over and grabbing the plate isn't okay. Please take that over again."

Is your child's whining a trigger for your yelling? If so, use the "Let's take that over" method when your child whines for her snack. "Jamie, you know how to ask for your snack in a different tone of voice. Please take that over, and this time use your friendly tone."

These four words become a simple way to remind your child to conform to some of the standards you have set for the family. Just be careful not to become a drill sergeant and insist on perfect posture and tonal expression all the time.

"Is There a Problem? Let's Figure It Out"

Say your little kids are in the kitchen fighting over who gets the last chocolate chip cookie. Instead of yelling at them to stop arguing, go into the kitchen and ask them what the problem is. There's a good chance they'll both say they should have the last cookie. Instead of offering to cut it in half, move the cookie aside and ask them if they have a solution. In this case it's pretty simple, and they will probably agree that cutting the cookie in half makes sense. This strategy helps you pause and consider what's going on, and it helps your kids put on their thinking caps to solve a problem.

Another example is a child who has forgotten to bring his school book home and realizes that he needs it to do his homework. He comes to you crying that he will get a bad grade because he doesn't have his book. Before you jump to rescue mode or yell at him for forgetting again, calmly say, "I see you have a problem. Let's figure it out."

Teach your child to take the following steps:

- Define the problem: "I don't have the book I need."

- Think of possible solutions: "I can borrow the book from Jessie down the block, or I can go back to school and see if it's still open. Maybe the janitor is there."

- Consider the consequences of each solution by asking, "What would happen if…?"

- Make a decision for a plan of action. "I'll borrow the book."

If you need to be involved with the solution (like driving back to school), you will take part in the decision. Otherwise, your child can make the decision himself. Afterward, talk about how it worked out. Problem solving is a great skill to learn at a young age. When challenges arise, help your child learn how to address the problem and be part of the solution.

Take Stock of the Skills You Have

You may possess some good skills you've learned from your work or training that you can repurpose for use with your kids. If you're a teacher by profession, you may know some good incentives for cooperation. If you are an executive in a corporation, you can use your leadership training and staff meeting skills to develop family meetings and schedules at home. If you're a nurse, you know about setting up care plans and thinking about the big picture. If you're a lawyer, you know how important it is to not get defensive and to stay calm even when you're not feeling that way. And if you're an artist, you can fall back on your creative nature when faced with uncertainty.

Too often parents lose track of what they know because of all there is to do. Stop, breathe, and come back to your wisdom. You have talents and skills to bring to your job as a parent.

A Thought to Consider:
I never realized there are so many options besides yelling.

Once you break the yelling habit, you will have more energy and attention to experiment with respectful ways to set limits and teach your children the skills they need.

Treating your children with positive regard and giving them positive feedback for their efforts is an essential part of a discipline plan. Children want to please their parents. They will notice the behaviors you approve of, even when they are not able to control their resistance to doing what you have asked.

Raising a family is like playing an instrument in a jazz band. It takes time to get good at it—you practice, improvise, take risks, get feedback, find your sound, learn the rhythms of others, and do your best.

Part 3

Special Circumstances

"It isn't what happens to us that makes us happy or unhappy; it is how the mind is set. What makes us suffer is the way we think about what is happening."

—Pema Chödrön, *No Time to Lose*

Innumerable special circumstances—illness, divorce, job loss—can increase yelling or challenge stability for you, for your partner, or for a family member. If this is the case, you may need additional support and understanding as you work to reduce your yelling.

Some people struggle because they live with a yeller and don't know what to do to help their partner or spouse stop. Your parents might yell at your kids when they come to visit or babysit, even though you've asked them not to.

Perhaps you or a family member has a mental health issue, neurobiological disorder, or chronic illness that compounds the likelihood of yelling. You may be facing challenging life circumstances such as divorce, the death of a loved one, or an abusive family member—all of which increase stress and, therefore, may increase the intensity or frequency of your yelling.

Shaming a relative who yells will only make things worse, and ignoring the problem isn't good for your children or your relationship with the yeller. Whatever your own special circumstances are, the chapters in this section offer you support. I encourage you to reach out to friends, family, or professionals when you are faced with difficult situations.

Chapter 8

"Help, I'm Not the Yeller"

Dealing with the Yeller
in Your Family

"I love my wife, but I'm starting to think she's harming our kids. She seems to think screaming is normal. I can't take the chaos any more!"

—Diego, father of a six-year-old son and
an eleven-year-old daughter

Families are complex combinations of individuals. You may not be the person in your family who yells; rather, you may be deeply affected by your partner's or family member's yelling habit.

In the classes I teach, it is not unusual for a person to "out" their partner who yells too much. I am always pleased when they are in the class together, knowing that both parents are interested in working to make changes. Sometimes only one parent is in class and sees yelling as a problem. When that is the case, it is difficult to change family patterns until both parents can agree on what's best for their child.

In this chapter we will also explore the complexities of having a relative react in a way that is counter to your values. It takes good communication skills to navigate the conversations that are needed so your children are provided respectful discipline from grandparents, aunts, and uncles.

We'll also address the question of when yelling becomes abusive, look at a variety of problems many families face, and learn strategies for dealing with them.

"My Spouse Thinks Yelling Is Normal"

Most parents find they have different temperaments from their partner or spouse. One person may be intense and reactive, and the other may be sensitive and cautious.

You and your spouse or partner may also have different parenting styles, with one of you being the giving-in, permissive type and the other being a lot like an army sergeant. Your partner may have been raised in a large family, where the culture of yelling was considered normal, while you were raised in a family where your parents never raised their voices, or vice versa.

Yelling at the kids may seem normal to your spouse because of the way he or she was disciplined as a child. Murray Straus and Carolyn Field (2003, 795) report, "Verbal attacks on children, like physical attacks, are so prevalent as to be just about universal." But just because frequent yelling occurs in many cultures, this does not mean that it is a healthy way to communicate with children. Your job is to explore how each of you was raised and to work together to come up with a plan based on your understanding of what your child needs and what you value.

Marta's Yelling Is Alienating Her Family

At a recent parent-teacher conference, Luis's teacher complained about his behavior. Luis, a twelve-year-old boy with high energy, was doing quite well academically, she explained to his mother, Marta; but he often teased and provoked the other kids in the classroom. He was disruptive to the lessons being taught. Although his behavior showed a lack of self-regulation, the teacher also thought Luis was smart and charming. The teacher mentioned that Luis might be bored, since he was ahead in his academics. When Marta began to cry because she was fed up with her son's behavior, the teacher suggested a temperament appointment with me.

Marta and her husband, Diego, came to a temperament counseling session together. Diego's attitude was "boys will be boys." He wasn't particularly worried about his son's behavior. Diego seemed proud of the fact that Luis was smart, funny, and outgoing. Diego himself is on the shy side, didn't do well at school, and didn't go to college.

Marta, on the other hand, was frustrated with Luis, especially since their daughter, Mari, was so well behaved at school and at home. Marta complained that Luis never listened to her and always tried to get his way. Every day he tried to talk his way out of doing his chores and homework. Luis's high energy, persistence, and intensity really got on Marta's nerves. She yelled at her son many times a day.

Marta was also intense, and her yelling became a habit that the other family members resented. Luis's sister, Mari, started to spend more time in her room listening to music and reading. She didn't like being around the yelling and arguing. Diego frequently told Marta to stop yelling at Luis, but that just increased her anger. Marta didn't want Luis to be disrespectful to his parents and teachers; she was never allowed to do that when she was a child. She didn't want to see her son go down the wrong path.

One day Diego came to an appointment with me without Marta. He expressed his feelings about his wife's yelling and said that it was causing increased tension between them. He was beginning to feel like he didn't respect his wife anymore, even though they had been together for fifteen years. He told me Marta had been calm with their daughter when she was young. He was sad to see how different his wife had become and wondered if maybe she was going through "her changes," since she was almost fifty. When I asked him if Marta understood how her yelling was impacting the family, he said no. He also admitted that they hadn't been spending time together talking or being intimate, so he didn't really know how she was feeling.

Marta and Diego Get Help

In the next meeting, I gave Marta and Diego some suggestions to help them deal with their differences, Marta's yelling, and the disharmony at home. If you are facing similar circumstances, perhaps these ideas can help you too.

Start With Your Relationship

I acknowledged Diego's feelings and reassured him that I could see how much love he had for his family. I stressed that working on his relationship with Marta would help their children, and I suggested ways to approach the distance he and Marta were experiencing.

- Consult a therapist for couples counseling. Although Diego was hesitant to see a therapist, he agreed that it was necessary. Marta's yelling was pulling them further apart, and they had lost their ability to communicate.

- Plan a weekly date night. Marta and Diego did not spend any relaxing or fun time together. They were always busy doing things for the kids or watching TV.

- Speak about your desires for the family. Diego was hesitant to tell Marta how he was feeling, and Marta didn't think he cared about her anymore. They both wanted more harmony at home but didn't know how to talk without blaming each other.

- Agree on ways to step in. Diego and Marta discussed how Diego could step in and help when he heard her yelling. Note: It's essential that this be discussed before an outburst of yelling. Having a plan that you agree on ahead of time will reduce the escalation that can occur if you intervene in a way that makes the yeller angrier.

- Assess the stress level of all family members. Diego realized that Marta was dealing with changes in her life and needed extra support. He was also under pressure at work. It was time for them to prioritize their commitments and activities and focus on each member of the family.

Look Through the Temperament Lens

When parents look at their relationship to their child from the perspective of temperament, they often get insight into their yelling behavior.

With some help, Marta and Diego were able to use tracking and temperament concepts to reduce the stress and conflict they were experiencing. You have the tools to do this as well. Become aware of the role that temperament plays, develop strategies, and reflect on the changes that are possible.

- Look at how your temperament interacts with that of other family members. Marta and Luis were both intense and persistent. Their similarities caused many power struggles. Luis's high energy and poor impulse control really triggered Marta. She compared Luis to his sister, who was very different in temperament. Mari usually did what her mother asked her to do. Marta's expectations for Luis were often unrealistic, and she didn't seem to recognize his strengths. Over time Marta realized that she needed to accept Luis's unique style and learn to help him channel his intensity into positive activities.

- Develop strategies based on temperament. Marta talked with the teacher about Luis's temperament and told her that Luis's nature is to want to be a leader and the center of attention. The teacher agreed to take Luis aside and praise him for his leadership abilities as well as to brainstorm a list of ways he could curb his disruptive behavior. The teacher decided to give him extra tasks to do, such as going to the office to pick up supplies and tutoring another student who was behind on work.

- Reflect on changes. Marta was willing to become more aware of her intensity and to see how quickly she yelled. Although she didn't think yelling was so bad, she understood that her daughter and husband were sensitive and that the yelling really bothered them. She also understood that she was easily frustrated by Luis and expected everything to be a problem. She agreed to work on her intensity and impulsivity in order to help her son with his.

Take Time for Communication and Connection

Diego introduced the idea of family meetings as a way to get the family back in connection with each other. Expressing appreciation was new for them. Positive feedback was not something anyone in the family was used to giving or getting on a regular basis. Over time and with practice, they took turns asking for what they needed from each other.

Diego realized that they hadn't had any fun together for some time and suggested they take a ferry ride and have a picnic the next weekend. Making plans and shining some light on the goodness of the family helped to shift the atmosphere at home. As Marta yelled less, Diego and the kids relaxed. And as Diego stepped up to the plate and became more involved with Luis's homework and chores, Marta became less reactive.

What You Can Do

In this example Marta and Diego were willing and able to get support from professionals. You may not have access to counseling or may not be able to afford it, or your partner may be unwilling to get professional help. In this case, I suggest that you have a heart-to-heart talk with "the yeller" and tell her or him how the yelling impacts you. Stay away from blaming language and stick to your feelings. Go back to chapter 6 and review the section "The Power of 'I' and 'You.'" Ask if you can read that chapter together, and let your partner know that you're willing to work hard on having things be more harmonious at home.

Reflect on what your partner may need from you or from others to move in the direction of change. In this example Marta needed a checkup with her physician to get support for her menopausal changes. Diego stepped in to help more with Luis's schoolwork and teach him ways to be less disruptive in the classroom. Luis wanted more time with his father, who has a calming effect on him. It's also essential to pay attention to the "quiet" child whose feelings may be ignored when there is so much going on with another child. Diego planned some outings with Mari. They liked bike riding and agreed to spend more time getting exercise and being in the outdoors together.

You can't make someone else stop yelling, but you can increase your compassion and focus your attention on what the other person is dealing with and needs. You can also model respectful communication, take on more of the household tasks, and do things to lighten the load of the other parent. You can also approach your partner with the idea of taking parenting classes together to gain a deeper understanding of normal growth and development of children. This will help you develop realistic expectations in responding to your child's behavior.

"Grandpa Yells at My Kids"

Responding to a situation where your children are being yelled at by their grandmother or grandfather is complex. Your reaction will be based on many factors, such as your relationship with your parents or in-laws, your philosophy of discipline, what the yeller actually says and does, the frequency of the yelling, the impact on your children, and your ability to communicate with all of the adults involved.

A grandparent's role is completely different than a parent's role, unless you're a grandparent who has taken on the primary caregiving role (see chapter 9).

I love my grandchildren deeply, and I also know that I am not responsible for their moral, cognitive, spiritual, emotional, and physical development. I can impact their development through my love and attention, but that influence is limited based on how often I see them. I learned early on that their parents are in charge; unless I see something that appears dangerous, I try to monitor and limit my advice. I say "try" because this is not always easy for me.

Sometimes my children ask for advice, and then they seem happy to hear my point of view. I respect the job they are doing as kind and attentive parents, so that also helps me respect their boundaries. When I take care of my grandsons, I do my best to follow the rules their parents have set forth. I discipline by setting limits, giving them choices, letting them know what to expect, and being patient. When I'm with them, I'm not busy doing other things, and so my full attention is available to them.

Having grandparents in your child's life is usually helpful and meaningful. When a grandparent's style and values are disruptive, however, some parents decide not to let the grandparents care for their children. If a grandparent is a yeller, you will need to face this difficult decision. It's important to weigh the advantages of your children having grandparents in their lives and the disadvantages of having someone yell at your children. If you see signs of neglect or abuse, it's essential that you take immediate action and not allow that person to care for your child, even if it is a grandfather or grandmother.

Getting Grandpa to Stop Yelling

Robbie is a single father of two boys, ages seven and ten. "I count on my father to watch my kids once a week when I have a class," he explains. "But he's a strict disciplinarian type who was raised with the idea that children should be seen and not heard. When the kids don't listen or when they question his rules, he yells at them. My younger son is afraid of Grandpa, just like I was as a kid, and doesn't want him to babysit anymore. I'm in a real bind. I know he's strict, but he also loves my kids."

Robbie's ex-wife is not involved in his children's lives, and he needs his father's support. He doesn't think his father is abusive, but he knows from his own experience growing up that his father has little tolerance for any sign of disrespect and will yell to get his point across.

In this case, Robbie was able to keep Grandpa as a babysitter by getting his father to agree to not yell as long as the kids promised to go to bed on time. Then Robbie put a reward system in place that helped the kids reduce their bedtime fussing. They could earn a weekend treat, like a pizza night or a movie, if they went to bed on time when Grandpa was there. Robbie told the boys and his father that he would check in with them each week to see if everyone was able to keep to their agreements.

What You Can Do

It makes sense that the person taking care of your children can discipline them if needed, but you need to define the type of discipline that you think is appropriate. You are the parent, and you have the responsibility to protect your children from fear and harm as best you can. Even though you may still yell at your child now and then, it doesn't mean that you should sanction someone else's yelling.

Here are ideas for working things out:

- Find out from your children what Grandpa says when he yells and what the circumstances are. Engage them in thinking about what they do before Grandpa yells that might set off his reaction. Their behavior may be triggering, but that still is not an excuse for Grandpa's yelling. Tell them you are sorry that he yells, and you will talk with Grandpa to work things out.

- Work with your children on strategies they can use to avoid Grandpa's yelling. Role-play with them to help them practice new skills.

- Let your children know how much you appreciate Grandpa's help and that you also understand how his yelling can be scary.

- Set up a time to talk with your father in person. Talking in person is always best. Start off by telling your father that you appreciate his help with the kids. Let him know you need to talk with him about his yelling and the kids' behavior.

- Listen to what your father has to say about babysitting and how things seem to be going from his perspective. You may need to do some personal inner work or deep breathing so your childhood memories don't overwhelm you and so you don't get defensive.

- Ask your father what circumstances cause him to yell. See if he is interested in working with you on the kids' behaviors he doesn't like so changes can be made.

- Tell him more about your philosophy and parenting style. Let him know that you are working hard to set limits and discipline without yelling and that you want his help.

- Ask him if he is willing to not yell at the kids. This is a key question. If he says yes, then you can go from there. You'll have to decide what your next step is if he says something like, "Yelling is good for the kids. Robbie, you're just letting them walk all over you." You can give him feedback about the impact yelling had on you and has on your children. He may or may not be willing to listen. The quality and content of your discussion will help you determine if you'll ask your father to babysit again.

- If he is interested in making changes, see if he would be willing to read this book. Brainstorm with him about changes that can be made.

- Let him know that when he watches the kids, he can discipline them, but yelling, name-calling, or physical punishment is not okay with you.

- Invite him over for dinner more frequently when you are home so he can have fun time with the kids and see how you implement your philosophy.

- If you sense that your father is not interested in changing, then offer to have him see the kids when you are around. Or, if you need him to continue to watch your kids until you can find someone else, ask him to please call you if the children misbehave, and you will handle it by phone. You'll need to work with the kids on their actions to keep things calm at bedtime.

Talking to your parents or in-laws about approaches to discipline is not an easy thing to do. It requires that you stand up for what you think is best for your children and speak honestly, even if you are afraid. It also calls for you to step back and think about your children's behavior and reflect on ways you can help them manage their impulses and become more cooperative.

"My Relatives Think My Daughter Is a Brat"

I have heard parents complain that grandparents or other relatives feel that they have the right to discipline their children harshly, even when the parents are right there. The acceptance of this approach varies from family to family, based on many things, including family values, culture, and boundaries that have been established and passed on from generation to generation.

In some families a child's behavior is fair game for any adult present to react to. They see a child as the responsibility of the entire family and want to be sure the child is respectful to all. If this is the case with your relatives and you don't agree with this approach, then it's time for some heart-to-heart conversations. It's important not to shame people in front of others, so unless it's an unsafe situation, wait till you can speak individually to your relatives when the kids are not present.

Rosy's Meltdowns

Maggie and her partner, Erin, have an intense, sensitive, active, and easily frustrated six-year-old daughter, Rosy, who always has meltdowns at big family events. At various times different relatives have criticized Maggie and Erin about Rosy's behavior and their "soft" parenting approach. More recently, Maggie's older brother yelled at Rosy to stop running around and being such a brat. Rosy left the room crying. It was hard to console her. When Rosy came out of the bedroom, her uncle apologized. He told her that she wasn't a brat but that she was making too much noise and he would appreciate it if she would stop.

Maggie and Erin were upset, and they made a few decisions that night after they got Rosy to bed. They wrote a letter to the family as a way to communicate their feelings and needs and to hopefully open the door for further conversations.

Dear family,

We are writing to ask you to please refrain from name-calling or yelling at Rosy. We know she is "spirited," often loud, and at times overwhelming. We ask that if you find you are getting stressed by or angry at Rosy, you come talk to either of us. We will deal with the situation and help her calm down or make better choices.

Sometimes it really helps Rosy calm down when you connect with her one-on-one. We've also noticed that she likes helping in the kitchen, so maybe next time she can help to make and serve dinner.

169

We really appreciate your love and look forward to getting together with everyone on Sundays. Please call if you want to discuss this with us. Rosy has started to work with an occupational therapist to help her be less reactive when she gets overstimulated. We would be happy to tell you more about this.

Love,

Erin and Maggie

Maggie and Erin decided that they wouldn't stay so long at family events, especially if Rosy was tired. Maggie was close to her younger sister, and they got together to talk about other ways to help everyone feel more comfortable. Maggie needed more support and a commitment from her family to be respectful and to understand Rosy's strengths and challenges. They had all accepted Erin into the family, and so she was hopeful that this letter would be well received.

What You Can Do

Not all families will be willing to address these kinds of issues. My advice is not to let your feelings toward your relatives get in the way of what you think is right for your child. Family is important, so do what you can to find solutions using healthy communication skills. If you feel criticized by your family, you won't enjoy yourself, and your perceptive child may also pick up on the tension and act out more. In the meantime, continue to assess your parenting style and see if you are setting clear enough limits or preparing your child adequately before going into situations where she may be overstimulated or overwhelmed.

If you can approach your child's grandmother, grandfather, aunt, or uncle with clarity and compassion, you have a better chance of being able to welcome his or her participation in the raising of your child. Together you can learn what it means to have your child's best interest in mind. Your family member's willingness to listen to you and work with you can bring healing to your relationship as well. There is no guarantee that your efforts will be well received. A family member may reject your point of view and pull back from connection with your child. It takes courage for you to attempt to work things out.

"My Partner's Yelling Seems Abusive"

If your spouse, partner, relative, or child's caregiver frequently yells at your child, your reaction will vary depending on many factors—your sensitivity, what the person says when he or she is yelling, the impact on your child, the intensity and duration of yelling, and the quality of the person's closeness and connection to the child.

Most parents yell sometimes. Losing it with a child now and then is not a sign that a person is a bad parent. Parents are under stress, and children test their parents' patience on a regular basis. Some children are more persistent and challenging than others. Some parents have more awareness of their emotions and have learned how to manage their strong feelings. Your imperfections are a part of who you are as a human being.

Is It Abuse?

Douglas Besharov (1990, 114), author of *Recognizing Child Abuse: A Guide for the Concerned,* says, "Emotional abuse is an assault on the child's psyche, just as physical abuse is an assault on the child's body." When a child is physically abused, there is often, but not always, a mark or a bruise to indicate that harm has come to the child. When emotional abuse occurs, it is difficult to see the immediate impact and to know how to protect a child. One definition of emotional abuse includes this: "The production of psychological and social deficits in the growth of a child as a result of behavior such as loud yelling, coarse and rude attitude, inattention, harsh criticism, and denigration of the child's personality" (Theoklitou, Kabitsis, and Kabitsi 2012, 64).

Based on their temperament, yelling may feel abusive to one child and not so much to another child. Your intense son might cry and yell, "You're the meanest mother in the world. I hate you!" because you calmly and firmly told him he couldn't stay up to watch a TV show that his friend is allowed to watch. His reaction might sound like someone just did something terrible to him, but his dramatic response doesn't indicate abuse.

As psychological maltreatment specialists Marla Brassard, Steven Hart, and Daniel Hardy (1993) say in their research, "The decision to label an action as emotionally abusive can be difficult because certain parental actions may upset a sensitive child, but may be appropriately administered to teach valuable lessons. Careful review of the overall interactions between the parent and the child, observation over time, and formal evaluation may be required before a pattern emerges" (720).

When is yelling considered abuse? This question is a real challenge. In my reading, talking with other professionals, and listening to parents, I've discovered divergent views on this issue. Some people feel that regular yelling is appropriate and necessary to discipline children. Other people think that intense and regular yelling is always abusive. There is no consensus as to when yelling should be considered abusive, because of all the variables. Most people agree that each circumstance needs to be evaluated on an individual basis and that the harm from yelling varies greatly in different situations and with different children.

The same question is debated when it comes to physical punishment. A light spank on a child's diapered bottom is different from hitting a child with a belt. There is a continuum of the intensity and impact of yelling. It's up to you as a parent to become aware of when a partner, spouse, or relative has crossed the line, so you can protect your child. Perhaps it's when your spouse's intensity, words, or actions are meant to hurt; when your partner no longer has a sense of your child's vulnerability; or when your mother has lost control and is venting her frustration and anger instead of providing discipline.

The Abuse of Power

I remember my intense anger on one occasion when my two youngest children were arguing. I could feel my cheeks getting warm, my body tensing, and my anger quickly escalating. Without any self-control, I began to yell loudly. I was so taken aback by the powerful emotions I expressed that I warned my children, "Leave the room RIGHT NOW!" I could sense in that moment that my anger was hurtful, and yet I couldn't calm down. My kids' fighting triggered me, but there were many other factors contributing to my emotional state that had nothing to do with my children's behavior. I don't remember the details of what else was going on for me at that time, but I still remember the physical sensations that accompanied my yelling. The feeling of being so out of control was frightening.

On reflection, I can see that the intensity of my yelling was an abuse of my power and energy. The looks on my children's faces were an indication of their fear and sense of threat. Because I was usually loving and kind, this event was doubly startling.

When Yelling Escalates in Intensity and Frequency

Toni is the mother of thirteen-year-old Margo and six-month-old Nikki. She says, "Whenever Margo and I have a disagreement or she complains about her chores, my husband, Luca, steps in and starts to yell and call her names. Luca's temper and harsh words are causing Margo to go to her friend's house most afternoons. I'm afraid that my husband's yelling has become abusive. He has started to curse and even threaten Margo with harsh punishment. I don't know what to do."

In this example, Toni recognizes that things are getting worse at home. Margo is feeling alienated from her mother and father, and Luca's loud yelling makes her angry and scared. Margo is dealing with increased stress caused by school expectations and the usual issues of adolescence. The whole family is still adjusting to the birth of Nikki. The baby wakes up crying a few times a night, so sleep deprivation is adding to the chaos they are all feeling. Baby Nikki seems to be crying more these days and clings to Toni all the time. Toni is anxious about what might happen next.

The Impact of Yelling on Babies

As I was writing this chapter, I heard about research by Alice M. Graham and colleagues, "What Sleeping Babies Hear: A Functional MRI Study of Interparental Conflict and Infants' Emotion Processing." The findings suggest that infants, when exposed to angry words, show a different brain response than when the same words are said in a neutral or fun way. This occurs even when they are asleep. "What we see for the infants in higher-conflict homes is that they are showing greater reactivity to the very angry tone of voice," the authors note, "and that reactivity is in brain regions that we think are important later on in terms of your ability to regulate your emotions and function well" (Graham, Fisher, and Pfeifer 2013, 782).

One question this research addresses is what impact parental conflict and angry speech (expressed by the adults' tones of voice) has on infants' brains and their future development. This study and others remind us that even babies are affected by the intensity and quality and frequency of yelling.

The Straw That Broke the Camel's Back

Toni's anxiety over Luca's yelling is warranted. Verbal abuse, like physical or sexual abuse, can be devastating and often leaves a child with lifelong scars. Verbal abuse can erode a child's healthy sense of herself and cause her to feel like she is bad or worthless.

The old saying "The straw that broke the camel's back" is from an Arabic proverb: "A camel was loaded to capacity, and the addition of just one more straw than it could carry broke its back" (Helterbran 2008, 56). The same can be said about the causes of yelling: when stresses are piled one on top of the other, just one small irritation can cause a person to explode. Ross W. Greene (2010, 91) says in the book *The Explosive Child*, "An explosive outburst—like other forms of maladaptive behavior—occurs when the cognitive demands being placed upon a person outstrip that person's capacity to respond adaptively."

Luca's Straw

Let's think about Luca's yelling and how he may have reached a breaking point with the stresses at home. Toni and Luca had never planned on having two children. When Toni discovered she was pregnant with Nikki, they thought long and hard about what it would mean to the family to have another child. In the end Luca supported Toni's decision to have the baby at age forty-two, even though his business was losing money, and he was really worried about how he would support the family. But the reality of the new baby was tougher than either of them had considered.

After Nikki was born, Luca worked longer hours, and he and Toni spent less time together. She wasn't ready to go back to work right away due to some health complications, and so it was difficult to balance the budget. Toni spent most of her time caring for Nikki and resting. Margo loved her baby sister but often felt ignored by her mother. Margo became more and more argumentative and rude, in part because she no longer had any time alone with her mother, and her father was no fun to be with anymore.

Margo was also starting to resent the requests to babysit when her mother needed to go to appointments or shopping. Luca was tired and felt unappreciated for how hard he was working. The increased yelling between Margo and Toni really set him off. He felt like he was carrying the load of responsibilities for the family and deserved to have some peace and quiet in his own home. He didn't want to yell at his wife, so he took his feelings out on his daughter, who was feisty and willing to yell back.

Your Challenge

When someone you love has become verbally abusive, your challenge is to understand how to be supportive of that person while at the same time protecting your child and yourself. That person, for whatever reason, can't cope with the demands being made on him from the environment, another person, or his internal taskmaster. If your family member is yelling more than once in a while, step back and think about the demands that are being made of this person you love and then begin talking together. Luca and Toni had a good marriage for many years. If they can get some respite—someone to help with the children on a regular basis—they may be able to treat each other and their children with respect. If they make the necessary efforts, they can get through this tough time.

The Yeller's Challenge

Luca's stress and frustration is not an excuse for his abusive yelling, but it is essential that both he and Toni recognize how his stress is driving his unhealthy reactions. His inner work is to become aware of his needs, his feelings, and his thoughts.

He can start by taking three or four deep, slow breaths when he hears his wife and daughter yelling, and then he can follow the other steps described in chapter 6. It may not seem like much, but if you make a conscious effort to take slow, easy breaths as you realize you are about to walk down the yelling path, you will give your brain chemicals a chance to shift. When you pause and breathe, your fight-or-flight reaction will begin to calm down. Then, you can think about another choice to make that isn't hurtful to your family.

Luca, like many people in his situation, has lost track of what he needs to balance his responsibilities to the family and his own health and well-being. Often people don't even have time to think about what they can do to change things. Perhaps one step is for Luca to take a day off, by himself, to rest and to think.

Get Help

If your partner or relative is out of control with yelling and it feels abusive to you or your child, get help.

In earlier chapters you reflected on the consequences of your yelling at your child. Take a moment now to sense once again how your child might feel when a person she loves is sending hateful words in her direction. Imagine how confusing that would be for a child and how it could rattle her sense of security and protection.

Your child will be frightened if he is a victim of your partner or spouse's abusive yelling, name calling, or rage. If this has been happening for some time, your child may have figured out coping skills to manage the feelings that he has to hold in and hide. If not attended to, these feelings can fester and be expressed in unpredictable ways. Potential consequences include depression, anxiety, eating disorders, self-harming behaviors, defiance, and aggression. Some children stop doing well at school, withdraw, or get in trouble. Others find ways to feel safe and find other adults to trust.

When a child has another adult in his life whom he looks up to, like a teacher or coach, that relationship can make a big difference in how resilient the child is in the face of parental conflict or abuse. Some children express their feelings through art, writing, or acting. Other healthy activities such as sports or caring for an animal can be vital outlets for a child.

Communicating that you want the family to get help is a good first step. Most likely, counseling is needed to help the family come together again and cope with their stress, feelings, and need for new communication skills. A class or book may help, but often that's not enough. Some parents have told me that their spouse was willing to seek professional help only when they put their foot down and said that they would no longer tolerate the way things were going. You don't have control over another person, but you can make decisions about your actions based on what you need and value.

If you live with someone who is verbally abusive to your child, you may also be a victim of this harsh and humiliating treatment. It needs to stop, and you need professional help to assist you in coming up with a plan that doesn't put you or your child at risk for further abuse. If you don't know how or where to get help, you can call the Childhelp National Child Abuse Hotline at 1-800-4-A-CHILD (1-800-422-4453). It is staffed twenty-four hours a day with professional crisis counselors. If your partner is being abusive toward you, you can call the National Domestic Violence Hotline at 1-800-799-SAFE (7233) to get advice and support. If you don't want to make a report, you can call anonymously to get information and to have someone to turn to.

You may experience tremendous shame if someone in your home is abusive. This shame can deter you from reaching out for help. Do not let it stop you. Do not downplay the impact of abusive behavior. We all need help sometimes. To change the negative patterns of abusive discipline or aggressive behavior, it is vital to find a professional who can work with your family: *everyone is suffering.* Breaking the cycle of abuse is vital for the health of your family and for future generations. A family member, friend, or religious leader can also help you find professional support and provide a compassionate ear to listen to your story. Reach out so you don't feel alone.

A Thought to Consider:
*I'm learning that I don't have
to tolerate other people's
out-of-control or offensive yelling.*

When you begin to become more aware of your thoughts, feelings, and actions, you will also become more attuned and able to look at other people and see how they affect you.

You and your children don't deserve to be victims of anyone's anger, hurtful actions, or abuse. It takes immense courage to face a situation honestly and to work toward finding a solution. Imagine what an advantage your child will have in her life if she can learn this from you. As you pause to breathe in and breathe out, notice how you can connect to the part of yourself that is strong, soft, and brave.

Chapter 9

"How Can I Stop Yelling When My Life Is So Challenging?"

Dealing with Difficult Situations, Disorders, and Differences

"I crave to be alone, to get just one full night's sleep, or to have one day without tantrums—but peace and quiet only comes in short spurts."

—Sheena, single mother of a child with special needs

If you are like most of us, there are probably times in your life when you feel like circumstances are out of control, unfair, or too demanding. You may feel like that for a day, a week, a month, or years. You have days when it's hard to get out of bed because of pain, exhaustion, or grief, but you do your best to function. Even if you want to run away and hibernate in a cave, you have the responsibility to treat your child as well as you are capable of doing, moment by moment and day by day. You won't always be thoughtful and patient, but you can come back to your intention of not yelling as you face the challenges that come your way.

Over the course of my career as a nurse, I've developed an understanding of the kinds of difficulties people face and the suffering they experience. As a temperament counselor, I have the privilege of listening to people tell their stories, which sometimes include trauma, pain, and loss, and I am impressed by the deep wells of courage and resilience that people call upon as they face adversity. I've come to understand that all families have problems to overcome. Some are obvious to others, like a child who has cancer; some may be less obvious, like a teen who has an eating disorder. Some families suffer more than others, but I don't know anyone who has raised children without hard times.

In his book *Man's Search for Meaning*, Viktor E. Frankl (2006, 112) (a psychiatrist and Holocaust survivor) says, "When we are no longer able to change a situation—think of an incurable disease such as inoperable cancer—we are challenged to change ourselves." The special circumstances in this chapter are situations you may not be able to change, but they must be faced. They are situations that are stressful and can easily trigger yelling. If that's the case for you, continue to be compassionate toward yourself and review the things you've learned in the other chapters. Think about how your situation affects your yelling and what you need to do to come back to your strength and place of knowing. As you face each day, regardless of what it brings, *you have the choice to stay aware of what you are feeling and thinking, and you have the choice not to yell at your children.*

Facing Divorce and Separation

"I know I shouldn't yell, but when my son comes home from his dad's house he disrespects me and challenges everything I say. I don't want him to think he can get away with that kind of behavior when he's with me."

—Miriam, mother of seven-year-old Rafi

When parents separate or get divorced, the entire family has to deal with many troubling emotions, including grief, shame, and anger. Many years ago, when my first husband and I separated and then divorced, I often felt conflicted about where to focus my attention. I needed support, while at the same time my children needed extra comfort, attention, and reassurance. Telling my children that their mom and dad were separating was one of the most painful experiences in my life.

There will be extra stress for everyone, even if both parents want the separation. It takes time for children to adjust—to new rules and schedules, to new ways of relating to their parents, and to the breakup of the family they thought was solid. Your child will work hard to accept what's new and different, while also feeling a deep desire to go back to the way things were.

Unexpected Help

Shortly after my first husband and I separated and I was living alone with my two children, my emotional life felt like a roller-coaster ride—with the downs of fear, sadness, and guilt taking turns with the highs of relief, adventure, and a newfound freedom. One stormy night I was in my bedroom crying, when my children came in to ask me to read them a story. I was completely involved in my sorrow and fear and said firmly, "Sorry, I can't read right now. Go and play until I'm ready."

My four-year-old daughter, who didn't take no for an answer very easily, kept asking me: "Please, Mommy, please, please read to us now." As I began to raise my voice and yell to get her to stop begging and to leave me alone, I looked in my son's eyes and down at the book he had picked for me to read. When I saw that it was Richard Bach's *Jonathan Livingston Seagull*, I knew that I had to put my feelings aside and comply with their request.

We snuggled on my bed, and as I read to them about a courageous, persistent bird, I knew that everything was going to be all right. I also learned that by focusing on my kids' needs, I was better able to manage my own reactive emotions.

Ways to Yell Less

As you work to yell less during a time of divorce or separation, you can rely on what you have learned in previous chapters. The tips offered here are specific to the challenges you are facing now or might face in the future.

- Be prepared for testing of rules and meltdowns when your child comes back to your house or leaves to be with his other parent. His behavior reflects his thoughts and feelings. Children need time to transition from one parent's house to the other.

- Have realistic expectations, and be patient as your child shifts gears. Yelling when you are frustrated with your child's behavior will create distance between you and slow down the reconnection process when she comes home.

- Work on routines for welcoming your child back to your house and for saying goodbye when he leaves. Perhaps you'll buy a special backpack or suitcase on wheels for a younger child. Part of your routine can be to help him pack and unpack. When your teen transitions home, you might give her a hug and then provide space for her to reconnect with her room, friends, or pet.

- Stay in communication. While your child is away, you might text each other goodnight or, you might send a young child off to his other parent's house with a little surprise or letter in his backpack. You can experiment with what helps your child learn to live in two homes. The more secure a child feels, the less he will act out and trigger your yelling.

- Do your best to not inundate your child with questions about what happened at the other parent's house. Kids don't want to be put in that position. If a child is interrogated, her anger may increase and be expressed through misbehavior.

- If you perceive or feel that your child is rejecting you, your hurt feelings may lead to yelling. If your child rejects your attention or requests, don't yell. Give him some space and time. Find ways to reconnect.

- Don't say bad things about the other parent. You are likely to have negative feelings about the other parent, but your child loves both parents. Don't put a child in the position of thinking she has to be loyal to one of you over the other.

- Set limits and rules. Your child will feel more secure if he knows what the limits are. Don't throw discipline out the door just because everyone is feeling bad. For example, if your son starts to text his friends during dinner, remind him that at your house, dinner is a phone-free zone. If he complains that his mom lets him text, just say something like, "Your mom and I have different rules. While you're here with me, no phones are allowed at the table. Let's talk about that book I saw you reading earlier." There will be times when you change some of the rules to accommodate new situations, but if you soften too much on limits, your children will test you more. If you and the other parent can agree to rules and limits, that will make it easier, but this is often not possible.

- Get relief from friends, family, or a babysitter if the other parent isn't able or willing to spend time with your child. If you don't take care of your needs, you will be more likely to yell. Find a regular, healthy outlet for your feelings.

- Pay attention to your own exaggerated reactions. Your child may remind you of the spouse who has left. As you notice the similarities, be sure to also focus on the differences so you don't take your feelings out on your child. For example, a father said to me, "I know my daughter's tantrums are normal. My ex-wife's tantrums, on the other hand, are not becoming of a grown woman, and they always make me mad. I'm trying to stay calm and not assume my daughter will grow up to be just like her mom."

Some parents report that they began yelling less frequently after a long-overdue separation or divorce. Tammy, a single mother of a twelve-year-old son told me, "I actually found that my yelling decreased when my partner and I separated. I realized after she moved out that much of the yelling at my son was really displaced anger at my ex-partner. I have found myself feeling a lot less angry and a lot more patient, now that I am out of the relationship." Tammy also noted that having "days off" when her ex-partner takes her son really helps her mood. She can catch up on sleep, chores, and work assignments. She's more attentive and rested when she's had time alone.

Keep Working at Yelling Less

One out of two marriages ends in divorce, so you are not alone in your journey to heal and recover from a relationship that is no longer healthy for you. If your yelling escalates, that's understandable. Forgive yourself, and keep coming back to the strategies in this book. Know that for most people, things get better with time.

There is much more to say about the impact divorce or separation has on you and your children. Many good books have been written on the subject of divorce, and I have listed some you may want to read in the resource section.

Don't forget to tell your child that the divorce isn't her fault. Often a child thinks that she did something wrong to cause the separation, and so she needs to hear you say (more than once) that it is adult issues causing the problems, not her. Listen to her concerns and provide extra love and affection.

The Challenges of Parenting Without a Partner

Diane, a single mother by choice, told me she was worried about her increased yelling. "When I had a roommate living with me, I definitely yelled less. I was more patient because I had an outlet for my feelings, as opposed to taking them out on my son." She was aware of her triggers but found that when she was the only adult at home she had a harder time managing her frustration and anger.

Some single parents entered into the parenting world with the intention of raising their child without a partner or spouse. Although they have made a conscious choice to parent alone, they often face the same challenges as other single parents.

And for most people, single parenting is not the ideal situation. It often comes after grief and loss due to a separation, the death of a partner, or an unplanned pregnancy. Many single parents find a new partner over time, while others parent alone during the child-rearing years. It's important to note that single parents often do a terrific job of raising healthy and happy children.

Catherine, a single mom, told me, "When I was raising an infant and a two-year-old alone, I was super stressed and sleep-deprived. I invented a mantra to recite when I started losing it and yelling. I'd say to myself, over and over: 'They are innocent; children are innocent; I am stronger than they are; I have more control than they do; I need to stay calm and together for them; they are innocent.' It really helped. In those moments of intense physical and emotional weakness, I needed to remind myself that I was the stronger one, and I was the protector. Getting in touch with this humbled me to the point of tears."

You May Yell More If...

Below are challenges you may face as a single parent and examples of some strategies to consider.

Challenge: You don't have someone to take over when your stress levels start to climb.

Try this: Exit the room instead of yelling—take a time-out for yourself. Turn on some music and breathe.

Challenge: You feel uncertain about what rules and limits to set and what consequences to impose.

Try this: Compare notes with other parents who have children of the same age. Have family meetings to clarify expectations and needs.

Challenge: Your daughter has difficult schoolwork that your partner used to help her with. You are unprepared and get angry every time she asks for help.

Try this: Notice that you are out of your comfort zone and consider getting a tutor or a friend to help out.

Challenge: Your children argue. Siblings can potentially become each other's targets for angry and hurt feelings.

Try this: Spend one-on-one time with each child. Listen to your children's feelings without the pressure to fix things. Assess if your children need someone else to talk with, especially if aggression toward a sibling is increasing.

Challenge: You have legal challenges with the other parent. You may lose your temper and say and hear things that fuel your anger.

Try this: Be sure to talk about these matters only when your children aren't around. Kids have big ears. Keep them from hearing things they shouldn't be hearing. It will only add fear and confusion to their already overloaded minds and hearts.

One of the only advantages that I recall as a single parent was that I didn't have to agree with another person about things such as discipline, bedtime, household rules, or weekend adventures. On the other hand, I did yell more when I was living alone. So I decided that finding friends to live with would be beneficial to my family.

After my separation and divorce, I learned a lot about myself. I faced deep-seated fears of being alone. I also discovered and developed strengths and capabilities that I could count on. I came to see that being alone was not the same as feeling lonely. I learned to count on others to help me raise my children. Learn what's best for you and your kids, and try to set up your life so you have the support you need.

Dino, a single father of teen daughters, told me, "It's essential as a single father to get time to connect with other parents to unload my stress, have some fun, and not feel so alone. I'm so unsure of how to raise my girls. I'm always yelling at them to stay safe and dress right. Sometimes I just want to put them in a castle, lock it, and throw away the key until they're ready for marriage."

If you live alone, reach out to friends to help you problem solve and to give you respite so you can have time for yourself. Check out your local community center or place of worship for single parents' groups or events. You can make friends who understand what you are dealing with. And you may be able to help another single parent with some of the basic survival techniques that you are learning.

The Hard Work of Foster Parents and Relative Caregivers

Foster parents and relative caregivers provide children with a supportive and safe family when children can't live with their birth parents. I have met many dedicated men and women who step in to help someone else's child, with little recognition or material benefit. Foster or relative care may be needed in cases of child abuse, neglect, incarceration, addiction, family violence, poverty, illness, death, teen pregnancy, or other unexpected circumstances. Some foster parents have extensive experience, support, and training, while others don't.

A relative caregiver may take on the responsibility of caring for a child because he or she feels that a child is better off with a relative than going into the foster care system. Aunts, big brothers, or grandparents may rescue a child from a harmful situation, even when their own health is poor or their finances are low.

Caring for someone else's child is always a complex venture and most often an act of compassion. Sometimes a foster home is temporary, and other times it becomes a forever home.

During a Kinship Care class that I taught, a grandmother told me, "I give so much, but my granddaughter doesn't seem to care about me. Can't she just behave?" Another foster parent said, "Once he saw how bad it was after spending a few days in juvenile hall, he turned his life around. He said, 'Mama, I want to live.' I was angry and afraid, but now I'm proud of him and happy that I never gave up."

If you are a foster parent or relative caregiver, it's normal to have mixed emotions about the circumstances you face. While wanting to be of service, you may also feel resentful and angry if you have to postpone some of your goals in order to care for a child. You may yell more frequently because of the stress you and those around you experience. If you aren't aware of the full range of your feelings and thoughts, you will be more likely to overreact and yell when a child challenges you.

Providing Discipline

Often, children who wind up in foster care or living with relatives have been traumatized. Children who have been traumatized will regularly exhibit behaviors that trigger their foster parents or caregivers. It's not unusual for children to exhibit testing behaviors to see if a caregiver or relative will accept them, even if they act out. Trauma ruptures trust, and a child who has been traumatized understandably loses trust in adults. A child needs time, consistent rules, kindness, and connection to begin to trust again.

Providing discipline as a foster parent or relative caregiver requires thought and practice so respect and trust can be built. Perhaps you learned during your foster care training that physical discipline and harsh punishment are not allowed. If you have used harsh punishment to discipline your biological children, one of your tasks is to learn new strategies. Because physical punishment isn't allowed, yelling often becomes a default discipline approach. Intense yelling may frighten a child, cause him to feel shame and withdraw, or stimulate aggressive behavior. Yelling will also cause your blood pressure to rise and will impact your health as well as your child's.

I have included books in the resource section that can help you discover positive discipline strategies beyond the ones you've learned in previous chapters. Experiment to find what works for you.

Reminders for Yelling Less

- Get enough sleep, get a checkup with your doctor, eat well, and exercise when you can.

- Find activities to do with your child that you enjoy, and set aside time just for the two of you.

- Talk to a friend, relative, or professional about your child's perplexing behavior. The child in your care is trying to make sense of what happened in the past, what to expect in the present, and what the future will bring.

- Recognize your limitations, and have realistic expectations. Carve out time to refuel.

- Plan ahead. Set priorities to keep up with appointments, homework, housework, bath time, meals, and chores—so you don't get exhausted.

- Notice the small things you are grateful for, and acknowledge the progress you and your child are making.

Caring for a child who has been traumatized or who has experienced loss is always challenging. Reach out for help. Check with local social service agencies or health professionals for resources. If you're not sure where to turn for help, call the National Parent Helpline: 855-4APARENT (855-427-2736).

Parenting a Child with a Disability, Delay, or Difference

If your child has a disorder such as depression, attention deficit/hyperactivity disorder (ADHD), a speech delay, a difference in learning style, or a disability such as autism, you're at risk for isolation, increased stress, yelling, and stigmatization. These differences are all on a continuum from mild to severe. The severity may be reduced over time with effective treatment and lifestyle changes.

The Stress of Stigma

Our society still has a long way to go in understanding and accepting the complexities of behavior based on genetic makeup, environmental factors, brain function, and human interactions. In the book *The Mark of Shame*, Stephen Hinshaw (2007, 242) reports on the pervasiveness of stigma when it comes to mental illness and disorders: "The most severe forms of mental illness receive major stigma, yet those experiencing and dealing with other types also confront rejection. For instance, caregivers of children with ADHD, high-functioning autism, and learning disorders are constantly reminded of the shortcomings of their offspring—and tacitly of their own parenting—at school, in social groups, and in public venues, often receiving considerable blame."

Chances are you have experienced pressure, and at times despair, because of what other people think about your child's behavior. Mina, a mother of a six-year-old son with autism, sat down in my office one day and sobbed. Her son had just had a meltdown in the hallway of the pediatric clinic. It had been a long, hard day, and when a nurse tried to get him to step onto the scale to be weighed, he lost it. He started to yell and kick, and then he ran out of the clinic. As Mina cried, she said, "I can't stand the looks from other people when my son is out of control. Their expressions seem to be saying that I'm a bad mother and if I would just yell at him or spank him, he would behave. They look at me with contempt. When this happens I just want to scream at him and beg him to act normal!" Mina, a devoted and compassionate mother, was exhausted.

Your child's behaviors can be embarrassing and perplexing. Your child may require more of your time and attention than other children. At times you'll feel like you are up against your limits. But because you are reading this, I know that you have a deep commitment to provide your child with guidance, love, and hope.

Learning Disabilities and Differences

If a child has a learning disability or learns differently compared to other children in his class, teachers and parents may become frustrated. This is especially true when a child's learning difficulty has not been identified or understood.

Learning disabilities are not caused by inadequate parenting or by poor educational experiences. *Nolo's IEP Guide: Learning Disabilities* states, "A learning disability is a problem taking in, processing, understanding, or expressing thoughts and information, as reflected in difficulties with reading, calculating, spelling, writing, understanding or expressing language, coordination, self-control, and/or social skill development" (Siegel 2011, 28). Explaining the differences between learning disabilities and learning differences is complex, because they mean different things to different people. The decision to use one term over another is often based on preference, level of impairment, or a need to make a diagnosis to obtain special education services.

Millie, like many parents who have a child with learning problems, yells during homework time. Although she knows her nine-year-old daughter, Kim, is trying to learn, Millie finds herself getting frustrated. "I start yelling when I have explained something over and over in many different ways but my daughter keeps asking the same questions over and over or daydreams."

Millie's desire to yell less has motivated her to find more support for Kim. For years she yelled at her daughter without understanding why her child wouldn't do her work like other kids her age. Finding out about Kim's learning disability has helped a lot. Recently, Millie asked the school for a new Individual Education Plan (IEP) and scheduled a meeting with the team to explore accommodations and extra tutoring. The teacher will tell Millie how long the homework should take and what to do when Kim doesn't understand the concepts.

Millie is doing her best to help her daughter without yelling, but she's often worn out by the end of the day. She suggests a new homework schedule for Kim—they will start homework right after dinner, before they are both tired and grouchy. Because of Kim's learning disability and attention problems, her mom needs to be nearby to get her started on her work, help her stay focused, and answer the stream of questions.

Your child may be average or above average in intelligence but wired in such a way that learning some subjects is quite difficult. When a child has a learning disability, you may not realize it until he is in school learning to read or write. If you see your child is frustrated with certain subjects or tasks, talk to the teacher to find out more. Request an evaluation as soon as possible. The better you understand how your child learns, the more able you will be to support his learning and reduce your yelling.

Think about the feelings that may underlie your frustration. Continue to notice your triggers and trace them to see if they are related to when you were in school. Did you struggle? Were people disappointed in you? Do you wonder why your son can't be an A student like you were?

Keep an open mind about your child's school or homework challenges. Children are smart in different ways. We all have our own strengths and areas of weakness. Look at what your child does well! Be your child's advocate with teachers and family members.

Ways to Yell Less and Help Your Child with Homework

- Plan ahead. Practice patience. Reduce distractions. Turn off phones and the TV.

- Ask your child to gather needed supplies and books before you begin.

- Be curious and engaged with your child's learning process.

- Focus on helping your child feel good about his mind and talents. Give positive feedback for efforts, not just results.

- End homework on a high note. Don't go past a predetermined amount of time.

Developmental Disabilities or Disorders

If you have a child with a developmental delay, you will need professional help to obtain services for your child and to assist you in understanding the meaning and implications of the delay. As with all of the special circumstances in this chapter, your child may experience a wide range of impairment. Your yelling and your ability to cope will be impacted by the severity of your child's disability or trauma and the amount of support you receive. Children with disabilities have many strengths. The more these strengths are recognized and encouraged, the more successful and happy your child will be.

Many years ago, I did a temperament assessment on a boy named Max who was asked to leave preschool because of his overreactive and aggressive behavior. I still remember his mother, Robin, well—in part because of her honesty as she expressed her feelings about the challenges she faced with her son. She was worried, confused, and triggered by his behavior. The teachers didn't understand Max and weren't supportive of Robin. They hinted that maybe something was going on at home that caused him to be so out of control. The teachers wanted the hitting and tantrums to stop, and when they didn't, Max was asked to leave the school.

I encouraged Robin to find a small, less stimulating child-care setting with a supportive staff. I also suggested Max be evaluated for a developmental delay or disability. Sometimes a particular school setting just isn't a good fit for a child, and once that child changes to a new school, things settle down. Unfortunately, this wasn't the case with Max.

The combination of his high sensitivity, poor impulse control, and difficulty communicating with other children were red flags. Robin knew in her heart that something was wrong with Max and agreed to get him evaluated. She and her husband were relieved to get a diagnosis—autism—even though they grieved deeply that something was wrong with their son that they couldn't fix. Max began to receive appropriate help for a child on the autistic spectrum. Robin's daily yelling stopped once she got support and learned more about what Max needed. She joined a support group where she could talk with other parents who really understood her and her son.

I stayed in touch with Robin. I was thrilled to learn that Max was doing really well in school many years later.

Attention Deficit/Hyperactivity Disorder

While working at Kaiser Permanente, I taught classes for parents of children who were being evaluated for attention deficit/hyperactivity disorder (ADHD).

Some parents left the first session of my class feeling sad that they had been hard on their children for being "bad." They began to understand that a child who is impulsive, unfocused, or hyperactive struggles to control his attention and actions. He may intend to wait his turn in line, for example, but his impulses won't let him. He pushes ahead of the other children. He hasn't learned yet how to put on the brakes.

Parents reported to me that they knew yelling was detrimental in the long run, but yelling seemed to be the only way to get their child's attention in the moment. Learning that their child might not have the necessary controls or focus made a big difference to these parents.

Burl couldn't understand why his stepdaughter, Jasmine, would agree to do something and then just not do it. Her second grade teacher complained that Jasmine spaced out during class and appeared to be in a world of her own. She often forgot to turn in her homework, which caused her grades to drop. Burl, an older father, had raised two other children who had always listened to him. He was frustrated with Jasmine, and yelling came easily to him. Burl was surprised when the pediatrician suggested he attend my class on ADHD.

The first thing he said to me was, "My daughter isn't hyper; she just won't listen to me, and that's not acceptable. She's got to learn to mind my words." After a few weeks Burl came to understand that his daughter might have the "inattentive" type of ADHD. Children who are diagnosed with inattentive ADHD often daydream, forget to turn in their homework, and procrastinate. They usually don't have trouble sitting still and tend to sit in the back of the room and not get in trouble. Jasmine was just like that, based on the reports from the teacher and parents. An evaluation and other tests were also done to rule out learning disabilities and a possible neurological disorder.

With some coaching, Burl began to change his expectations and put some simple strategies in place.

- He no longer called to her from the other room when he wanted her to do something.

- He gave her one instruction at a time and made sure she completed it before he asked her to do something else.

- They made an evening schedule, and if she completed all of her work on time, they would read one of her favorite books together.

- Burl met with the teacher to get Jasmine's seat changed from the back of the room to the front. The teacher also had some ideas for helping her pay attention, such as using colorful markers and asking her to participate in discussions more often.

Burl was willing to try different discipline approaches at home, in part because he realized that yelling wasn't working. He came to see that Jasmine wanted to do the right thing, and she appreciated his help. He also focused on her talents more. He arranged for the guitar lessons she had been asking for once she was able to turn her homework in on time on a regular basis.

Becoming educated about ADHD is the first thing to do to help reduce your frustration with a child who has trouble focusing and controlling impulsivity. Medication is only one possible aspect of treatment, and many parents try other things to help reduce their child's impairment before they make a decision about medication. Each situation is different, so work with a professional you trust. At this time there is no blood test or scan to confirm a diagnosis of ADHD, so find a professional who is experienced, spends the needed time evaluating your child, takes a good history, and includes the teacher's observations in the evaluation.

Some parents in my classes admitted that they too had attention and impulsivity issues, which added to the yelling and chaos at home. Most parents never got the help they needed. Their child's struggles motivated them to get help for everyone in the family.

Emotional Disorders and Mental Illness

Parents often have limited knowledge of their child's inner emotional world and the challenges they face. A parent may think that a child is just being lazy when she wants to stay in bed or just being moody when she cries a lot, when she may actually be suffering from depression. When a ten-year-old says he won't go to school because he's too scared of taking a test and is sure he will faint in class, his parents may think he is faking it. Yelling doesn't address his underlying impairment and fear. His parents don't understand the depth of his anxiety.

Your child will experience a wide range of normal behaviors based on her temperament, environment, and developmental stage. Sometimes, though, her behavior means there is more going on that needs your attention. It isn't effective to yell, "Eat your dinner" at a teen suffering from anorexia. A child who won't go to school unless all of his trains are lined up in the same exact order every morning won't change his compulsive habit just because you get angry and yell.

Disorders such as schizophrenia and bipolar disorder, or chronic illnesses such as diabetes or severe asthma, take extraordinary emotional resources on your part. Continue to develop your ability to stay calm in the face of emotional turmoil. And continue to find professionals and friends you trust to talk to and cry with.

If you are yelling a lot and are perplexed by your child's behavior, it's a sign that you need another set of eyes and ears to help you figure out what's wrong and what to do.

Seeking Professional Help

If possible, start your inquiry into finding help early, before things get overwhelming. Even if your cultural norms encourage not going outside of the family with problems, there is no shame in needing help. It's vital to remember that all families face hard times. If your child had an injury, you would seek treatment from a medical professional without hesitation. There are so many choices and confusion about what your child needs when it comes to learning and mental health issues. Sometimes people hesitate because they don't know where to find help.

Begin with Someone You Trust

I frequently suggest that parents begin seeking help by making an appointment with their child's pediatrician or family doctor. Schedule a checkup to rule out any medical problems. A child might be identified by a teacher as one who can't pay attention due to restlessness when she really only needs glasses. A child who is taking too much asthma medication may be irritable and appear to be hyperactive.

After the appointment, arrange a time to talk by phone or in person with your child's doctor in private. Tell her your concerns, find out what suggestions she has, and ask whom she recommends and why. If you don't have a doctor who is sensitive to school or emotional issues, then look elsewhere. I've worked with terrific pediatricians who are attuned to the complex needs of children, but there are some doctors who may dismiss your concerns. Don't let that stop you. Trust your intuitive sense that something is wrong, and find a professional who will listen.

Do your research about different types of therapy, and ask the professional you talk with to explain the advantages of his or her approach.

If your child is having learning problems, start with your child's teacher to get as much information as you can. The school may tell you that there is a long wait for an evaluation for learning disabilities, but keep going. Put your requests for an evaluation in writing (the date is important), and find an advocacy group in your community to help you understand the process of getting testing done. There are helpful books to guide you through the process as well. Sometimes parents go to a private psychologist for educational testing. There is a high cost for this, but many people who can afford it find it faster than relying on the school. You want to be sure that the school will accept the report from a private psychologist if special education services are needed. This is a complex subject and too extensive to cover here, so find someone who knows the laws to guide you.

You may need more than one professional to support your child. There may be an occupational therapist (OT) that helps to treat a child on the autistic spectrum. A speech pathologist might work with a child who has a language delay. A psychologist or behavioral pediatrician may diagnose conditions such as ADHD, anxiety disorder, or depression. A licensed clinical social worker (LCSW) or a marriage and family therapist (MFT) may run groups for teens with bipolar disorder or provide play therapy to a young child coping with the loss of a parent. A pediatrician or child psychiatrist can prescribe medications when that's part of the treatment plan. A nurse or health educator may offer classes in mindfulness or parenting skills, and a learning specialist may provide tutoring. Some people seek help from alternative practitioners such as acupuncturists or doctors who have studied herbs or homeopathy.

Explore the treatment options through books and reputable websites, friends, and relatives. Keep your particular child in mind, knowing that what works for one person may not be right for another. Find out how much experience the professional has. If you need low-cost therapy and are working at a clinic or with an intern, find out the background of the person who supervises the intern. Explore how you can be involved in the treatment, since you need to learn new ways of helping your child.

If a professional doesn't treat you respectfully, pushes you to do something you are not comfortable with, or avoids your questions, get another opinion. You are a vital part of the team. Take a friend or relative with you for support when you go to school meetings, and always ask questions. Ask to talk about your child's strengths as well as struggles.

Much of the care covered by insurance is based on a medical model of treating behaviors or symptoms to make a diagnosis. Be sure any professional you go to takes a good history in order to understand the many factors that contribute to your child's behavior. Knowing that a favorite dog died months ago may be a key factor in understanding a child's sadness. Your child may be experiencing grief rather than showing signs of clinical depression.

Getting help when things are tough is essential for your work on yelling less. With information and understanding, you will discover new ways to treat your child. The support you receive will also serve to reduce your isolation and lighten your load.

But don't let the time you spend researching the right treatments interfere with the time you have with your child. Your love is good medicine no professional can provide.

A Thought to Consider:
Yelling doesn't help difficult situations get better.

If only we could protect our children and ourselves from all suffering and pain! We can't, but we can do our best to manage stressful situations that throw us off balance. Yelling doesn't make anything better; it only takes you further away.

We all make mistakes as parents and miss clues pointing the way toward healing. When your kids are grown, you will look back and realize the things you could have done differently—if only you had been more aware, knowledgeable, courageous, or kind. Forgive yourself for mistakes you've made, and do what you can now to make a difficult situation a little bit easier. Spend a few minutes each day thinking about the things you are grateful for. This will help you restore your balance during hard times.

Epilogue

World Peace Begins at Home

Imagine a world in which

- there are no wars;

- people resolve conflicts by talking to each other and coming to agreements for the benefit of all;

- no one goes hungry or is without a home;

- there are free child-care centers with well-paid, loving staff;

- the core school curriculum includes lessons in kindness, generosity, empathy, community service, nature, and climate health;

- a child's love of music, art, dance, and discovery is valued in school;

- all neighborhoods are places where children are safe to play outdoors, and there is no fear of violence;

- when children are young, the community provides for parents so they can bond with their children;

- every neighborhood has a community garden;

- all children are happy, healthy, and cooperative.

The words *world peace begins at home* came to me many years ago in response to the question of how we can have a more peaceful world. I imagined what it would be like if everyone saw their parental role and actions as a piece of the world-peace puzzle.

Usually, I feel optimistic about life. I can tune out the bad news and focus on the good things. But not always. Sometimes a sense of hopelessness creeps into my normal positive attitude. To help me change my emotional state, I give myself the same advice I would give you: "Do what you can ... start small ... breathe ... don't worry ... have faith ... practice generosity ... laugh ... love ... start with yourself." In this way I remind myself to come back to what is possible.

Recently, I noticed that I also feel hopeful when I meet with parents who are doing their best to understand themselves and their child, when I teach a class to child-care providers who love their job and want to learn as much as they can, when I watch parents laughing and playing with their children, and when I see my adult children working to make their world better.

When we do our best to treat our children, others, and ourselves with kindness and respect—even with our imperfections—there is a ripple effect. A shift takes place in ourselves, in our children, in the people we interact with every day. When we heal our wounds with courage and honesty, we can use our energy for our benefit and the benefit of others. One person—like you or me—can have a significant impact on the violence, greed, suffering, and lack of compassion around us all. If more parents model respectful communication and empathy, then the next generation will have a better chance to create a more peaceful world.

Consider these questions every day:

- What will I discover today that brings meaning to my life?

- What will I learn from my children, and what will they learn from me?

- How can I offer love, comfort, or peace to someone?

Discovering the answers will bring you joy.

***

Thank you for reading *Is That Me Yelling?* Please let me know what aspects of the book are meaningful to you and what questions you have. You can reach me through my website, http://www.nurserona.com.

May you be safe, healthy, happy, and successful in your desire to yell less.

With gratitude to all parents everywhere,

Rona Renner

Acknowledgments

As I read my manuscript I am reminded again of the parents who shared their stories with me in classes, on the radio, in their homes, and wherever we met. (I have changed the names and other identifying information to maintain confidentiality.) There have been hundreds of professionals, friends, and family members who have influenced my current understanding. It's because of all of them that I was able to write this book. Thank you.

A heartfelt thanks to the parents in my Yelling Less focus group who provided invaluable early help: Sevran, Nina, Rhonda, Darlene, Jill, Tamara, and Kristen.

I am forever grateful to my husband, Mick, who, with humor, encouragement, thoughtful editing, foot massages, and a willingness to do whatever is needed has helped me accomplish my most challenging goals.

I am blessed to have found Naomi Lucks, a writing coach who held my hand throughout the proposal and book-writing process. I'm grateful to another coach, Carolyn Foster, who helped me discover the focus for this book.

Twenty years ago, I was fortunate to meet Matthew McKay, PhD, author, psychologist, and cofounder of New Harbinger Publications. I learned many of the concepts in this book from him. At New Harbinger Publications, thank you to Tesilya Hanauer for believing in my book, and to Jess Beebe and freelancer Gretel Hakanson for your support and editing skills.

When I began working at Kaiser Permanente, Richmond Medical Center, in 1991, my professional path took a new turn. Mel Burman, MD (the best boss ever), asked me to participate in a Kaiser Temperament

Project where I met James Cameron, PhD, and learned about temperament. Jim continues to be my mentor. I also had the privilege of learning from temperament pioneers Stella Chess, MD, and Alexander Thomas, MD. My gratitude to other temperament professionals: David Rosen, MD; David Rice, PhD; William E. Carey, MD; Sean McDevitt, PhD; and Mary Sheedy Kurcinka. My appreciation to Jan Kristal, MA, and Helen Neville, RN, who coauthored the *Instructor's Manual for Temperament-Based Parenting Classes* with me as part of an innovative collaboration between Kaiser Permanente and the Preventive Ounce.

My gratitude to Peter B. Collins, Hillary Flynn, Susan Lindheim, MD, and the other board members who helped me start the nonprofit organization that produced the *Childhood Matters* radio show. And thank you to the thousands of guests and callers who shared their wisdom with me on the airwaves. Muchos gracias, Marisol Muñoz-Kiehne, PhD, for a thousand things and for writing a bilingual parenting column with me for many years.

My deep appreciation for the teachers who enhanced my ability to write this book. Phyllis Pay, founder of the Intuitive Energy Center, told me five years ago that there was a book inside of me waiting to be written. Over the years the women in our Tuesday-night meetings have supported my efforts to become more familiar with myself. I am also grateful to Isa Gucciardi, PhD, director of the Foundation of the Sacred Stream—a school that provides abundant opportunities to learn. And thank you to Ronald Aguilera, who helped me understand more about myself and the value of honest communication.

A special thanks to my current inspirational village: Christine Carter, Ralph Singer, Tom Widlinger, Jan Camp, Barry Barkan, Charlene Leung, Will Courtenay, Jason Brand, Michelle Larager, Phil Catalfo, Rosy Aronson, Savita Skye, Mark Friedman, Rocio de Mateo Smith, Carolyn North, Rebecca Wood Breen, Julie Kurtz, Intisar Shareef, and Jorge Partida. Special thanks to Felsha Zuschlag for being such a shining light in the world!

Thank you to my daughters-in-law, Marsha Rose and Jennifer Renner, for your love and sense of humor, and to my son-in-law, Andrew Bray, for being there when I needed advice. My gratitude to my sister, Maj Kalfus, and brother, Bart Feder, for telling me to write a book and for being creative people and thoughtful parents. Thank you, my dear mother, Florrie, for your "You can do it" attitude and enthusiastic spirit, and my stepfather, Stan, for showing up just when you were needed.

And I end this book where I started, by thanking my children—Carina, Matt, Mara, and Pay—my love for all of you has been the key motivating factor in this journey to learn how to be a good mother. Thank you for your love. And thank you to my grandchildren, David and Maceo, for reminding me how precious childhood is.

Appendix

Meditations

Audio versions of all of these meditations are available online at http://www.newharbinger.com/29071. See the back of the book for more details about how to access them.

Self-Compassion Meditation

This self-compassion meditation came to me when I was writing this book and feelings of self-criticism were popping up.

> Sit down in a comfortable place, in a chair or on a cushion, or lie on the floor.
>
> Gently close your eyes. Become aware of your breath. Notice your breath—breathing in and breathing out. There is no need to change your breath—just notice it with each inhalation and exhalation. Become aware of your body, sense your body, and scan your body for any places that have tension from your toes all the way up to your head. Notice any places of tension—your neck, shoulders, jaw, or hands. Keep your awareness on your body and on your breath.
>
> Now, imagine holding yourself as a baby. You were once an innocent, beautiful baby.
>
> Notice your size. Look at your hands, look at your feet, look at your face, and become aware of your expression. Babies show their emotions without hesitation.
>
> Does your baby look content? Curious? Sad? Afraid? Joyful? Sleepy? Take your time and notice your baby's face.
>
> Are you aware of your baby without judgment? With full acceptance? You may want to rock your baby gently in your arms. How does he or she respond to your gentle touch?

You may want to bring your baby close to your chest, patting him or her gently.

If your baby is experiencing any pain or suffering, you can provide comfort. Sense: how do you care for your baby? And if you want to, you can bring your baby into your heart and surround him or her with love and light.

Sense how you and this baby are one. Take another minute to feel kindness toward your baby and toward yourself.

If you want to, you can now picture the child or children you are raising, and sense the kindness and love you feel for them. They were once babies as well—soft and innocent newborns who came into this world to be cared for by you.

Now, if you choose to, you can expand the circle of kindness to include other people you love or know, or people who may be suffering physically, emotionally, or spiritually.

Know that you can feel this kindness toward yourself anytime. When you make a mistake, yell too much, disappoint someone, or lose something valuable, you can feel compassion and acceptance of yourself as you would for a baby who was crying. You can let go of self-criticism; you can let go for right now.

If you notice any judgments, let them go, as you get ready to transition from your experience with your baby.

Now, bring your attention to the sounds around you. What do you hear? When you are ready, gently open your eyes and notice the light, shapes, and objects in your room.

May you feel compassion and acceptance for yourself and others. And may your compassion remind others of this possibility.

Tree Meditation

This meditation is dedicated to the liquidambar tree outside my window.

When you are ready, find a place to sit on a chair or pillow, or if you prefer, you can lie down. If you sit in a chair, place your feet on the floor, loosen any tight clothing, sit with your spine straight, and feel your weight on the earth. If you are lying down, sense the floor, mat, or bed below your body.

If you are comfortable doing so, close your eyes and begin to bring awareness to your breath. Notice your breath—breathing in and breathing out. Some people like to breathe in through their nose and then out through their mouth. It's up to you. You can just notice the natural rhythm of your breath. Such a gift, your breath is bringing life to your entire body, breathing in and breathing out, here in this moment. In this moment in time, there is no need to do anything except notice your breathing. When thoughts come to mind, notice them, without judgment, and then let them go.

I invite you now to imagine that you are a tree. You are strong and beautiful. You may be large with a wide trunk and have branches reaching to the sky. Or you may be a small, delicate tree, bending with ease as the wind blows. Picture the shape of the leaves. Are they like the five-pointed-star of the liquidambar, or are they mighty like a palm tree?

Sensing your feet, imagine your strong roots below the surface, bringing you nourishment. These roots ground you and help you be secure. Now, bring your attention up into your legs, past your ankles into your lower legs, into your knees, into your upper legs. Become aware of your pelvis, hips, and abdomen. Bring your attention to the place where your body meets the chair or the floor or the bed below you. Continue to notice your breathing as you become aware of your chest. Your lungs are expanding and relaxing, breathing in and breathing out. Become aware of your back. Like a tree, you are strong in your trunk and able to withstand all kinds of conditions around you. No matter if it is raining or snowing or the wind is blowing or the sun is shining, your trunk will stay strong.

Now, bring your attention to your shoulders and then down into both of your arms, hands, and all of your fingers. Your hands are like the branches of a tree that move and sway and reach to the sky.

Become aware of your neck and your jaw, and notice if there is any tension. If so, bring your breath to any areas of discomfort in your neck or in any part of your body. Your breath can meet the tension and offer some relief. Become aware of your head, face, and hair, and picture beautiful and strong branches with leaves of any color and shape reaching from the top of your head to the sky. These leaves will come and go with the seasons, and the tree will grow as long as it gets water and sun and stays rooted to the earth, which provides it with nourishment. With the seasons the tree changes, growing new leaves and shedding old ones. As you feel your strength and beauty, imagine how being a parent requires you to be strong and flexible, and like the tree, you shelter small creatures from the storm. And like the leaves of the tree, you shed old ideas and grow new ones.

When you are ready, sense your body, and now bring your attention to the sounds around you. What do you hear? Cars? An airplane? A dog? Notice the sounds.

And now, when you are ready, slowly open your eyes and look around you. Take in the light, notice the objects—ordinary things that may look different now. As you move from this state of mind and body, remember how it feels; at any time during the day, you can remember and benefit from the strength, presence, and beauty of your tree.

May your roots keep you secure, your trunk keep you strong, your branches keep you flexible, and your leaves bring you and others happiness.

Resources

The following is a good selection of many beneficial resources you can use to complement what you have learned in this book. Please visit http://www.newharbinger.com/29071 for a more extensive list.

Selected Books

Aron, Elaine N. 2002. *The Highly Sensitive Child*. New York: Broadway Books.

Badalament, John J. 2010. *The Modern Dad's Dilemma*. Novato, CA: New World Library.

Bailey, Becky A. 2000. *Easy to Love, Difficult to Discipline*. New York: HarperCollins.

Bardake, Nancy. 2012. *Mindful Birthing*. New York: HarperCollins.

Brach, Tara. 2003. *Radical Acceptance*. New York: Bantam Books.

Brassard, Marla Ruth. 1987. *Emotional Abuse: Words Can Hurt*. Chicago: National Committee for Prevention of Child Abuse.

Brazelton, T. Berry, and Joshua D. Sparrow. 2006. *Touchpoints: Birth to 3: Your Child's Emotional and Behavioral Development*. Cambridge, MA: Da Capo Press.

Brown, Brené. 2010. *The Gifts of Imperfection*. Center City, MN: Hazelden.

Carter, Christine. 2010. *Raising Happiness*. New York: Random House.

Chopra, Deepak. 1997. *The Seven Spiritual Laws for Parents*. New York: Three Rivers Press.

Chödrön, Pema. 2001. *The Places That Scare You*. Boston: Shambala Publications.

Eifert, George H., Matthew McKay, and John. P. Forsyth. 2006. *ACT on Life not on Anger*. Oakland, CA: New Harbinger Publications.

Elkind, David. 2007. *The Power of Play*. Philadelphia: Da Capo Press.

Germer, Christopher K. 2009. *The Mindful Path to Self-Compassion*. New York: Guilford Press.

Gordon, Mary. 2009. *Roots of Empathy*. New York: The Experiment, LLC.

Greene, Ross W. 2010. *The Explosive Child*. Rev. and updated ed. New York: Harper.

Hallowell, Edward M. 2002. *The Childhood Roots of Adult Happiness*. New York: The Ballantine Publishing Group.

Hannibal, Mary Ellen. 2007. *Good Parenting Through Your Divorce*. New York: Marlowe & Company.

Kabat-Zinn, Myla, and Jon Kabat-Zinn. 1997. *Everyday Blessings*. New York: Hyperion.

Kabat-Zinn, Jon. 2012. *Mindfulness for Beginners*. Boulder, CO: Sounds True, Inc.

Kurcinka, Mary Sheedy. 2000. *Kids, Parents, and Power Struggles*. New York: HarperCollins.

Kurcinka, Mary Sheedy. 1998. *Raising Your Spirited Child*. New York: HarperCollins.

Levine, Madeline. 2012. *Teach Your Children Well*. New York: HarperCollins.

MacKenzie, Robert. J. 2001. *Setting Limits with Your Strong-Willed Child*. New York: Three Rivers Press.

McKay, Matthew, Patrick Fanning, Dana Landis, and Kim Paleg. 1996. *When Anger Hurts Your Kids*. Oakland, CA: New Harbinger Publications.

Neff, Kristin. 2011. *Self-Compassion*. New York: HarperCollins.

Neville, Helen. 2007. *Is This a Phase?* Seattle: Parenting Press.

Rettew, David. 2013. *Child Temperment*. New York: W. W. Norton & Company.

Siegel, Daniel. 2012. *The Whole-Brain Child*. New York: Bantam.

Siegel, Daniel. 2003. *Parenting from the Inside Out.* New York: Penguin Group.

Smith, Jeremy Adam. 2009. *The Daddy Shift.* Boston: Beacon Press.

Shure, Myrna. 1994. *Raising a Thinking Child.* New York: Simon & Schuster.

Weissbluth, Marc. 2003. *Healthy Sleep Habits, Happy Child.* New York: Ballantine Books.

Websites

Temperament

The Preventive Ounce: http://www.preventiveoz.org

Understanding Behavioral Individuality: http://www.b-di.com

Other Parenting Sites

American Academy of Pediatrics: http://www.aap.org

American Psychological Association: http://www.apa.org

BabyCenter: http://www.babycenter.com

Common Sense Media: http://www.commonsensemedia.org

Dr. Hallowell, ADHD expert: http://www.drhallowell.com

Dr. Toy (advice on children's products): http://www.drtoy.com

Greater Good Science Center: http://www.greatergood.berkeley.edu

KidsHealth: http://www.kidshealth.org

Kids in the House: http://www.kidsinthehouse.com

Zero to Three: http://www.zerotothree.org

References

Barkley, R. 2000. *Taking Charge of ADHD*. New York: Guilford Press.

Besharov, D. 1990. *Recognizing Child Abuse*. New York: Free Press.

Brach, T. 2003. *Radical Acceptance*. New York: Bantam.

Brassard, M. R., S. N. Hart, and D. B. Hardy. "The Psychological Maltreatment Rating Scales." *Child Abuse and Neglect* 17 (1993): 715–29.

Brown, B. 2010. *The Gifts of Imperfection*. Center City, MN: Hazelden.

Cameron, J., and Rice, D. General Impressions of Your Child's Temperment, 1994.

Cannon, W. B. 1915. *Bodily Changes in Pain, Hunger, Fear and Rage*. London: Appleton-Century-Crofts.

Chess, S., H. G. Birch, and A. Thomas. 1977. *Your Child Is a Person*. London: Penguin Books.

Chess, S., and A. Thomas. 1986. *Temperament in Clinical Practice*. New York: Guilford Press.

Cohen, S., D. A. J. Tyrrell, and A. P. Smith. "Psychological stress and Susceptibility to the Common Cold." *New England Journal of Medicine* 325 (1991): 606–12.

Cohen, S., W. J. Doyle, E. Frank, J. M. Gwaltney Jr., B. S. Rabin, and D. P. Skoner. "Types of Stressors That Increase Susceptibility to the Common Cold in Healthy Adults." *Health Psychology* 17, no. 3 (May 1998): 214–23.

Courtenay, W. H. 2011. *Dying to Be Men*. New York: Routledge.

Engel, B. 2002. *The Power of Apology*. San Francisco: Wiley Press.

Frankl, V. E. 2006. *Man's Search for Meaning Paperback*. Boston: Beacon Press.

Germer, C. K. 2009. *The Mindful Path to Self-Compassion*. New York: Guilford Press.

Graham, A. M., P. A. Fisher, and J. H. Pfeifer. "What Sleeping Babies Hear." *Psychological Science* 24, no. 5 (2013): 782.

Greene, R. W. 2010. *The Explosive Child*. Rev. and updated ed. New York: Harper Paperbacks.

Greenspan, S. 1996. *The Challenging Child*. Cambridge, MA: Da Capo Press.

Hallowell, E. 2006. *CrazyBusy*. New York: Ballantine Books.

Helterbran, V. R. 2008. *Exploring Idioms*. Gainesville, FL: Maupin House Publishing.

Hinshaw, S. P. 2007. *The Mark of Shame*. New York: Oxford University Press.

Kabat-Zinn, J. 1990. *Full Catastrophe Living*. New York: Delacorte Press.

Kurcinka, M. S. 2000. *Kids, Parents, and Power Struggles*. New York: HarperCollins.

Lamott, A. 1999. *Traveling Mercies*. New York: Anchor Books.

McKay, M., P. Fanning, D. Landis, and K. Paleg. 1996. *When Anger Hurts Your Kids*. Oakland, CA: New Harbinger Publications.

McKay, M., P. D. Rogers, and J. McKay. 2003. *When Anger Hurts*. 2nd ed. Oakland, CA: New Harbinger Publications.

Meltzer, L. J., and J. A. Mindell. "Relationships Between Child Sleep Disturbances and Maternal Sleep, Mood, and Parenting Stress." *Journal of Family Psychology* 21 (2007): 67–73.

Neff, K. 2011. *Self-Compassion*. New York: William Morrow.

Nelsen, J., L. Lott, and H. S. Glenn. 2007. *Positive Discipline A–Z*. 3rd ed. New York: Three Rivers Press.

Phelan, T. W. 2010. *1-2-3 Magic*. Rev. 4th ed. Chicago: ParentMagic, Inc.

Shure, M. B. 2005. *Thinking Parent, Thinking Child*. New York: McGraw-Hill.

Siegel, L. M. 2011. *Nolo's IEP Guide: Learning Disabilities*, 5th ed. Berkeley, CA: Nolo Press.

Straus, M. A., and C. J. Field. "Psychological Aggression by American Parents." *Journal of Marriage and Family* 65 (2003): 795–807.

Tesser, A., R. Forehand, G. Brody, and N. Long. "Conflict: The Role of Calm and Angry Parent-Child Discussion in Adolescent Adjustment." *Journal of Social and Clinical Psychology* 8, no. 3 (1989): 317–30.

Theoklitou, D., N. Kabitisis, and A. Kabitsi. "Physical and Emotional Abuse of Primary School Children by Teachers." *Child Abuse and Neglect* 36, no. 1 (2012): 64–70.

Verbrugge, L. M. 1985. "Gender and Health." *Journal of Health and Social Behavior* 26, no. 3 (September 1985): 156–82.

Verbrugge, L. M. 1989. "The Twain Meet." *Journal of Health and Social Behavior* 30, no. 3 (September 1989): 282–304.

Photograph by Kids in the House

Rona Renner, RN, graduated from Brooklyn College School of Nursing in 1966, and she has since been dedicated to solving problems and helping people reduce their suffering. Her extensive experience includes working in medical hospitals and mental health programs in New York City and California; training women in childbirth preparation in Zaire, Africa (now the Democratic Republic of the Congo); helping to start a learning disabilities program in Pune, India; and providing parent education and ADHD and temperament counseling at Kaiser Permanente in Northern California. Renner was the founder of the *Childhood Matters* and *Nuestros Niños* call-in parenting radio shows, and hosted the *Childhood Matters* radio show for ten years. She currently consults and teaches classes for mental health professionals, teachers, and parents throughout the San Francisco Bay Area and beyond. Her greatest teachers have been her four children, two grandsons, and her husband Mick. She lives in Berkeley, CA. To learn more, visit nurserona.com.

Foreword writer **Christine Carter, PhD**, is a happiness expert, sociologist, and the author of *Raising Happiness: 10 Simple Steps for More Joyful Kids and Happier Parents*. Carter has helped thousands of people find more joy in their lives through her books, online classes, coaching, and speaking engagements. She teaches happiness classes online throughout the year to a global audience on her website www.christinecarter.com. Her blog is syndicated on the *Huffington Post* and *Psychology Today*.

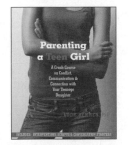
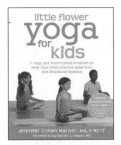
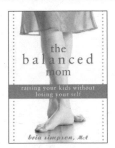